The Complete Approach

A Scientific and Metaphysical Guide
to The Paranormal

The Complete Approach

A Scientific and Metaphysical Guide to The Paranormal

Barry FitzGerald and Dustin J. Pari

Summer Wind Press

Attica, New York

The Complete Approach

ISBN 978-0-692-00462-3

Cover Design by Jeffrey Ouimette

Dedication

I would like to dedicate this book to my lovely wife
Diane, our boys Nathan and Jake, and our beautiful
daughter, known affectionately as "Beans." You are the
loves of my life – always know that everything I do is
for you and you alone. ~ Dustin

Acknowledgments

Dustin J. Pari

There have been a lot of people who have helped me throughout the years, so I do hope for the forgiveness of having such an extensive list.

First and foremost I would like to thank God for all the blessings he has bestowed upon me, and whom I will faithfully serve until my last breath. I would like to thank my parents for always sacrificing so that I would never have to go without, for raising me in a home filled with love and for always being there to listen and to guide.

I would like to thank my closest circle of friends: Richard Fredette, Dennis Ventetuolo, Paul Jones, Pete Cardoso, and Joey D'Antonio for always being there and having my back as we have grown together through the years. You truly are the best friends a guy could have. To my long time friend Darren Valedofsky, thanks for walking the road with me from elementary school to the grave and for always being supportive without question. I would walk into the mouth of hell to fight the Devil himself as long as you were with me.

To my dear Uncle Bub for inspiring me to write and for teaching me how to survive life in shades of gray; never fully conforming, never truly being off the grid, but walking that line in the middle.

Very humble thanks to Father Roger Durand for helping me to find my way back to God and to eternal salvation.

My appreciation goes out to all those in the paranormal field whom I have had the distinct pleasure of working with throughout the years. Thanks to all the fans, friends, and fellow researchers who have been kind enough to talk with me, share with me, and dream with me, as we struggle to prove what we all know is true.

A special thanks to Marc Tetlow from Ideal Event Management for his dedication to this and all my projects, for his true friendship, and belief in my ideas. Thanks to Joe Rose from Abrams Artists for guiding me through the legal world of contracts and entertainment law.

To my long-time friend and editor of this project, Erik "Baldman" Scalavino – your friendship to me throughout the years is rivaled only by your compassion for mankind. My sincere thanks for helping shape and mold my rough-around-the edges thoughts.

To Jeff Ouimette, the designer of this handsome book cover, thanks for always being a dear and true friend, always willing to go that extra mile, and always being there for me and for my family.

To my dear friend, fellow paranormal researcher, and co-author Mister Barry FitzGerald. Thanks for helping to write this magnificent piece of work, for your friendship, your tutelage, your trust, and for all the laughs we share on the road. Many a time I think I would have quit and headed for home if not for your support during our travels abroad. God truly does love the Irish, and with good reason.

Thanks to Nathan and Jake for being two responsible and loving young men that any man would be happy to call his sons. Thanks for looking closely after your Mom and your sister while I am away. I am so very proud of both of you.

To "Beans", who is truly "Daddy's little girl" — you are everything that is beautiful in this world to me, and more. I am amazed at everything you have already done, and your life is just beginning. I pray you will live a long, blessed, and charmed life and always know that Daddy loves you.

And lastly, but most importantly I would like to thank my wife Diane for being a pillar of strength, hope, comfort, and love. For believing in me, when even I had questioned my abilities. For always welcoming me home with a warm embrace, a passionate kiss, and a plate full of delicious chicken cutlets. You truly are my one and only love, now and forever — thanks for making my life complete.

Barry Fitzgerald

I would like to give my special thanks to Dustin J. Pari, who drove me to help produce this publication and share the vast amount of information found inside, which has been accumulated over the years. I have the greatest of respect for his friendship and core values that he holds dear and I can only tip my Irish hat to this truly committed husband and father.

I would also like to thank my family for their continued support as I travel the globe visiting every new location and experience the true nature of the paranormal. Putting the finishing accounts to this publication, I was sitting by the window of the apartment in Argentina and was stopped in my tracks to witness a truly spectacular sunset, which left me in awe and thanks at witnessing such a phenomenon.

A special thanks goes tour Marc Tetlow, our manager of events for both Dustin and I who can be contacted at marc@iemanagment.com and who worked as our manager for this publication. And, thank you to Rob Thompson of Summer Wind Press, our publisher who stuck by us as we worked in areas that presented great difficulty in communication to get this publication to the public.

But of course I cannot forget the teams and individuals I have worked with out there in the field, those people whose interest and dedication have brought them to this point. I truly thank them for their support and work they have presented to this field of research, which has not been an easy one. Some of my sources have long been forgotten in my notes, which span twenty years, but I still acknowledge their work and dedication to the field.

In the memorable words of Leonard Nimoy in his famous role as Spock: "Live long and prosper."

Foreword

A word from Barry

My name is Barry FitzGerald and, after 18 years, I would see myself as a seasoned researcher and take much of my experiences from the ability to travel to other countries and understand the similarities in many paranormal phenomena that surrounds this planet. The ability to work with others from other countries and perspectives has allowed me to develop this mass of knowledge and now put it to print and share with the rest of the paranormal world. My hat must come off in memory of good researchers from days gone by whose very work has led to this publication.

Many of us have made sacrifices to better our understanding and help generations to follow. Even today, I still have a great wonderment with many aspects of the paranormal. New entities have been discovered and our understanding of these is increasing on a yearly basis; we must remember that this does take time and cannot be rushed. Deceit, sleight of hand, and smoke screens are part and parcel of this hunt for the truth and, from my viewpoint, make the game much more challenging and certainly not a bore.

But I remind myself on a daily basis never to lose sight, always to keep my guard. And to you, the reader, I urge you to be careful and not to underestimate this field. It's not a research subject that should be taken lightly, as mistakes - some of which can rip families and lives apart - - are common in this uncertain science.

I hope by contributing to this publication we can at least light the way somewhat and avoid the pitfalls which have swallowed many before us.

A word from Dustin

I am Dustin Pari, an investigator into the paranormal realm for over 16 years as of this writing. Over the course of those years, I have seen and heard things that would make most people not only believe in spirits and apparitions, but also question the very essence of their own being.

I am involved in the field of paranormal research for a very simple reason: to give proof to the world that there is definitely some sort of afterlife, some accountability for our actions, so that, in turn, we will all live better lives and treat each other with more respect. I really would like to be part of the team, or even an inspiration to the team, who finally makes that bridge to the other side. Hell, I will even settle for being on this planet when this happens, just to witness the reaction of it all.

I cannot imagine the impact that this event is going to have someday in the whole world. Of course, until everyone can adapt and understand that, in essence, what we are proving is that all are one, it will cause religious riots, controversy, and looting.

Looting? Yes, looting. People love to feel justified in stealing a plasma television.

It is my personal belief, based on my experiences in the field, in life, and in deep thought, that in fact, all life is truly connected and that our energies never die. In death, we simply move on to the next level, which is for the most part, currently unseen. Yet some of these energies can dance incredibly close to that line, and in some cases, cross over to make contact.

Whatever the reason for all of this may be, when we are finally able to make regular contact with the next level, when we are able to get enough proof to make everyone realize what is truly going on, it is going to be the most remarkable breakthrough and discovery of all time.

I do hope that we finally are able to prove what so many have known as truth for so long -- that this life is not the end, that our achievement of the next life hinges in part upon this one, and perhaps, just maybe, we can all be a little bit nicer to each other while we are here.

Perhaps by publishing my thoughts and knowledge, I may be able to further inspire the person who makes this dream into a reality. In the meantime, stay vigilant, keep on trying new ideas, and keep the faith.

We are much closer than we think.

Table of Contents

This book has been designed and
written by researchers for researchers.

Chapter 1

Getting to Know Your Ghosts

Types of Entities

"It's not what you look at that matters, it's what you see."

HENRY DAVID THOREAU

Poltergeist Haunting:

"They're heeeerrrre…"

This, from the hit film Poltergeist, is quite possibly one of the most famous lines from a movie about the paranormal. But don't believe everything you see in movies.

Poltergeist activity is mostly noted for its seemingly spontaneous first appearance and then its just as sudden disappearance. It should be noted, however, that not all cases are as cut-and-dried, or as quickly passing as they may seem.

The most popular theory that remains today is that an individual, better known as the "agent" in terms of poltergeist cases, may actually manifest the activity. They themselves develop and manifest activity due to an unknown or subconscious psycho kinesis (PK).

Common agents include women going through menopause, as well as teenage boys and girls going through the age-old transition of puberty.

More on the agents and the contributing factors in a bit; for now, let us focus upon understanding some of the common types of poltergeist activity for better identification within the field.

Psycho kinesis is quiet simply defined as the movement of physical objects by the mind without use of physical means or manipulation.

This differs from telekinesis, as that is better described as the production of motion in objects without contact or other physical means as in manipulation done consciously, a purposely-produced action. Think spoon bending -- that is a good example of telekinesis.

PK is the movement of objects by oneself without his or her knowledge that it is happening. Objects suddenly sliding across the kitchen floor would be alarming even to the poltergeist agents, as they don't realize it's possibly their own mental doing.

Object manipulation is not limited to that of a poltergeist type activity, nor is the agent theory the only explanation for poltergeist activity. Intelligent Spirits and Inhumans are both able to manipulate objects at will and sometimes in response to an investigator's request. Therefore it is imperative that other determining factors are taken into consideration before writing off a possible haunting as a simple biologically induced or hormone-fueled side effect.

According to some case studies, poltergeist phenomena seem to happen gradually, increasing in their severity as they continue and usually going dormant for a period of time after manifestation. The poltergeist usually starts affecting your senses, such as smells and small visual disturbances, or perhaps disembodied voices or the sound of rapping on a wall. It may increase over time to include visible moving shadows, mischievous behavior such as hiding one's personal belongings, doors opening and closing, electrical disturbances; towards the end of the cycle, it can increase to pinching, slapping, banging, movement of heavier objects, and in very rare cases, some have reported audible communicative voices.

This energy or spirit is by no means new to the field, nor really is it a true spirit. The name originates from the German poltern, which simply means noise or rumble, and geist, meaning ghost or spirit. One of the earliest accounts of a poltergeist appears in a pamphlet from 1698 and can be seen in the British Museum (London) describing stones and various other objects being thrown.

It is amazing to see the listings of accounts of such a manifestation appear all over the world and over different time periods from 1797, 1817, 1849, 1926, and right up to present day. It is also very interesting to see that various EMF (Electro Magnetic Field) have been reported, ultra- and infra-sonic sounds have been recorded on location, as well as ionized air.

The theory of infrasound, a sound too deep to be heard by the human ear, was first introduced by the late Mr. Vic Tandy of Coventry University in England. Although infrasound in nature is not dangerous, it has been manipulated by mankind to make weapons such as those experimented with by French researcher professor Vladimir Gavreau in Marseilles.

The professor always felt ill at work but discovered that the recurrent attacks of nausea only bothered him when he was in his office at the top floor of the building. Using devices sensitive to various chemicals, he tried to track down what may be disturbing him and his fellow workers, but he discovered instead the whole room was vibrating at a very long frequency. The source to the energy turned out to be an air conditioning unit on the roof. The professor was amazed and excited by his findings and their obvious potential and developed machines to produce infrasound so he could investigate it further. One particular machine was described to resemble a huge police whistle and was powered by compressed air. The technician gave the giant whistle its first blast but it is alleged he fell dead on the spot. A post-mortem revealed that all his internal organs had been vibrated so severely that they mashed to jelly. Readers can gather more information on this tantalizing subject from Gerry Vassilatos, author of 'The Sonic Weapon of Vladimir Gavreau.'

The effects of infrasound can also include visions of ghosts and the terror that ultimately comes with them. Everyday things, such as wind moaning around a building or even a car engine that can create a standing wave, can cause the low frequency waves. We may not hear them but scientists have known for years that they can affect our bodies physically and emotionally.

These standing waves can be explained in physics and can cause vibrations and a dash of physiology explains the effects on the body.

The symptoms begin with a feeling of being uncomfortable with your surroundings, feeling cold, and sweating. The sound wave causes the eyeball to vibrate in sympathy and so blurs the vision at the edges of the eye and leads the victim to breathe heavily. This then triggers feelings of fear and anxiety, which in turn will make the victim hyperventilate.

Usually the images reported are those of someone standing or moving and will have been created by an object or a small movement in the periphery of their sight. The mind will fill in the rest. Direct vision will make the phenomenon disappear. NASA Technical report 199770013810 mentions a resonant frequency for the eye at 18Hz. Another Technical report, 19870046176, mentions hyperventilation as a whole body vibration. It would be prudent of those who wish to research the Paranormal to examine this if you are on a case. We have experienced this phenomenon and even though we were aware of it there wasn't a damn thing we could do to shake the fear, which engulfs you. Vibrations constantly surround us, but most times our body is simply not even aware. Take for instance a violin that is left on a table. It will always hum to itself gently, and this is true with all matter, as all matter vibrates.

In the case of the Rosenheim Poltergeist in Germany in 1968, physicist F. Karger from the Max-Planck-Institut für Plasmaphysik and G. Zicha from the Technical University of Munich found none of these effects present, which has puzzled researchers for a long time. So the debate still rages on where the poltergeist phenomenon originates. [We would advise our readers to chase up a copy of the Hutchison effect online, which will give you a better understanding of what to look out for should you ever be involved with a poltergeist case.]

Within Dr. John Hutchison's lab experiments in Canada it has been reported that the activity which mimics the poltergeist ranges from moving objects, objects being thrown across a room, metals being disrupted at the molecular level, mysterious fires and of course levitation of objects, these objects can be made of paper, plastic, metal and wood.

There is no telling how long the phenomena will take to complete a cycle -- whether it takes a day, 3 months, or a number of years -- and there is no telling how long it will stay dormant before it starts another cycle. But within the lab it was interesting to note that when high levels of EMF were present, nothing seemed to happen until a human subject entered the lab. It seems we are the catalyst for such activity.

The first and number-one way to decrease and get rid of Poltergeist phenomena is through licensed therapy. It is usually turmoil and/or drastic stress that bring on the poltergeist phenomena. So having the agent(s) go through necessary therapy to alleviate their personal stresses and turmoil will usually slow down or stop poltergeist activity from happening. Also there are very few cases out of the thousands where the agents have nothing going on in their lives. It is trauma and stress that the energies feed on and the more the teenager has in his or her life, the more apt they are to invite poltergeist activity, whether they are causing it themselves or not.

Residual Haunting:

One of the most common types of "ghostly" activity is the residual haunting. These are the shadows of what once was, playing out again and again in current time. A residual haunting or sightings primarily occur in the same place by definition alone, hence, the reoccurring event.

These apparitions of people and things from the past are stuck almost in a time loop, appearing most often at the same time of day in the same place. They do not appear to acknowledge the presence of people from today's time, nor are they confined by the current place-ment of objects. They can appear to walk through walls, following a path from the past when such walls may not have existed.

The spirit itself isn't really even there. Only the im-pression and the energy exist, stuck in this time loop. Picture it as an old videotape running over and over again.

The paths traced by the energies are usually those that the spirit was most familiar with during its time. For example, some are said to have been seen walking down old country road sides once traveled heavily by people from past times.

Other times it can be that the energy is trapped due to some event, which can sometimes even be a replay of their last moments on this earth. This is common in instances of suicides or violent and brutal murders. It is as if the energy becomes part of the surrounding area in which it was most familiar or from which it was most tragically ripped. However not all residuals are due to tragedy, as we will further explore.

The residual haunting isn't usually bound to the current state of the dwelling or space, but somehow attached to the land or area itself. This is why such "ghosts" may appear to be walking through walls -- in their time, a passageway existed there.

Some people are of the opinion that a residual haunting is a sensory phenomenon that can be attributed to a traumatic or life-altering event, like an echo of past events. We have found there is no such reason for this to happen; it can simply come to be. A residual can be a recording of a happy event just as much as a traumatic one.

Take this case that Barry personally worked on.

Gillhall house, built in 1670 in County Down, was known as the most haunted house in Ireland. Its only competition, 'Leap Castle,' lay in County Offaly. Legend and local tales had the spirits of the house walking the estate and sending fearful mortals fleeing from its walls.

The local paranormal group Barry was associated with acquired permission from the new owners of the estate to execute a series of experiments (based on new research on which Barry was working). After some time had elapsed, Scientific Paranormal Research (SPR), based in County Down, took over the experiments and brought them to a close the following July. The ultimate goals of the experiments were to determine what events led the locals to assume the estate was indeed haunted.

First, the group had to examine the records of the estate and meet with people who worked in and around the house. Sheila St. Clair was part of a group that examined the house during the 1960s and her notes where vital if the case was to proceed. The BBC accompanying Sheila made a series of recordings within the house. The recordings captured ranged from sounds of raging fires, thumping, banging, and heavy engines being revved. Sheila was adamant no one else was in the building as she had posted watchmen outside, ruling out the possibility of human interference.

The sounds were once again echoing. It was suggested in some circles the crystal found in some types of stone recorded the sound, then played it back after a lengthy interval of time, but the trigger mechanism for the events remained unknown.

The history of the estate proved enlightening. A castle stood on Greenan Hill approximately ½ mile from the site of the house and predated it by about 200 years. Could the stone from the castle have been used in the construction of the house, resulting in contamination from another building?

Recorded history indicated this might have been the case. John MaGill in 1670 reduced a castle in Rathfriland in County Down to build houses and he may have done the same at Gillhall. The original house was extended and improved in 1731 by Robert Hawkins MaGill and some of the remaining stone may have been taken from the castle site in order to complete this task.

Needing more proof for their theories, SPR arranged a meeting with men in Wales who executed experiments that produced sound from walls inside an old County Court. The same types of experiments were also carried out in Germany after the Second World War. The information gathered backed up the theories SPR had and led to a series of tests to produce the same effects experienced in Wales and Germany.

SPR interviewed gentlemen who served in the Royal Air Force (RAF) based in Gillhall during WWII and discovered they belonged to the Royal Engineers Corps, who subsequently worked on heavy engines producing large amounts of revving on the estate.

After relentless research over the course of the next several months, SPR believed they had found the key for the events. On a hunch, the group organized equipment on the bridge which spans the river Lagan leading to the location of the house. At 3:35am on the morning of July 26, 1998, a carriage was heard approaching from the rear entrance. Correlating information forwarded by the British Geological Society in London and Edinburgh, it emerged there was an earthquake in the North Mid Atlantic Ridge at 3:38 a.m.

SPR believed this was the key. Before an earthquake, the Earth's Electro Magnetic Fields rise significantly and these fields trigger the sound to replay. SPR believe certain areas around the world are connected by these means, which could explain the noise heard by many people at these sites.

They concluded that what we do and say may under certain circumstances be recorded and when the environmental factors are correct, these sounds are played back. In the case of Gillhall, if we were recorded we have now become the ghosts of Gillhall. Understanding that sometimes the residual can be simply a capture or echo of the past can greatly help clients rest in their own homes. There is no ill intent behind it, there is no reasoning, it's simply is.

Most residuals just seem to be happily caught up in the routines of what they did in their daily lives -- paths trodden over and over that have somehow left an energy signature that is recurring. Walking up and down stairs, opening doors, going to bed, or even cleaning up rooms are some of the most common residual haunting sightings.

This type of haunting poses no threat to those of us alive today, which is good because there really is not much you can do to make them go away. Some believe that by altering the landscape or dwelling, they will release these faded apparitions. However the best thing you can do is come to terms with it and acknowledge it for what it is.

It is often beneficial upon finding a residual to note the exact date and time that it occurs as many do follow a very strict pattern in regards to when they will appear, some even being only once a year, where others could be every day at 7 in the evening. Noting these times is important so that they may be studied again over a period of time for further possible identification.

Residuals make for a good investigation as they are somewhat predictable and are not affected by your presence. Their scheduled appearances also make it much easier to capture them on film or video -- so keep a strict journal of appearance times and get your cameras ready.

Intelligent Haunting:

The term "Intelligent Spirit" has absolutely nothing to do with the IQ of the spirit itself, nor that of the person investigating it. It simply means that it possesses the ability to interact with us, the living.

Many ill-willed Inhumans will masquerade as a simple Intelligent Spirit, the difference being that the Intelligent Spirit, like you and me, was at one time alive, where as the Inhuman was not, (see more on Inhuman trickery in the Inhuman chapter).

In comparison to the Residual haunting, which has no awareness of the living in this time, the Intelligent haunting is somehow able to communicate with us through various means such as Electrical Voice Phenomena (EVP) recording and object manipulation.

We are still in the process of understanding exactly how it is possible for some of those who have passed on to cross over and communicate with us and there are new theories popping up all the time. Perhaps through your own study and investigations, you will develop and possibly even prove a theory of your own.

These Intelligent Spirits can be either negative or positive in their response to an investigator and can even be different in their responses to various team members.

The most impressive aspect of investigating the claim of an Intelligent Spirit lies in its ability to interact.

Among the oldest and simplest means of communication is the "knock once for yes, twice for no" back-and-forth, in which the investigator poses a verbal question with the simple request of a knock in reply.

When using this method it is important to check for false positives by asking the same question repeatedly, also to ensure that the "answers" were not merely coincidental. In addition, we recommend that you familiarize yourself with your surroundings and the environmental factors that may contribute to ambient sound within the investigation area.

This knock-in-response method can also be achieved by using an EMF (Electro Magnetic Field) or TriField meter with an audible indicator. You simply introduce the meter into the room or area and verbalize to the spirit or spirits what you are intending to do, what the meter does, and how you would like them to use it, by moving near them and manipulating the energy fields to create a sound.

The beauty of investigating an Intelligent Spirit is that a very intimate connection can be made. Spirits have been known not only to provide answers to questions on digital voice recorders in the form of an EVP, but they will sometimes actually have enough energy to speak aloud in what is known as a Disembodied Voice.

There is something to be said about hearing a voice of someone who you know is not present with you. It can bring chills to your spine and possibly tears to your eyes. This type of connection and interaction is rare in comparison to capturing an EVP or a knock/EMF type response.

If you are given an idea whom the spirit may have been when it was alive, you can call to it by name and direct your line of questioning towards something particular to that person or its time. This type of specificity will increase your chances of capturing some type of response.

Death is not the end; it's a new beginning. Though some choose to remain, and this can be for any number of reasons, such as a natural attraction to a place or even a murder victim or the murderer. Countless reasons exist for a spirit to remain, yet only a small amount do, in the purest sense and in connection with a haunting.

Mediums state spirits surround us. This we don't doubt, but those have freedom to come and go. Sometimes you will get one that remains in a location. Of course, then the question arises of our spiritual duty to release the spirit from the location. But for now we will address the case at hand and deal with the matter of gathering evidence of such an event occurring on location or inside a home.

As in death, it seems these mirages of former owners or friends have emotions such as humor, concern, sometimes determination, drive, and hate. They were once alive, and understanding your entity can help greatly in bridging that divide to allow communication to occur.

The next time you are walking in a supermarket or down the street, make eye contact with ten people, smile and nod your head that you acknowledge they are there and move on. Note how many don't respond in kind. This is very true in the world of spirit as well, but how many would have responded had you not made the attempt first?

Making the attempt is important and respecting your entity is just as important. The EVP questions you use to reach your entity should be asked out of respect, not simply thrown out there with no feeling behind them.

Imagine you are face to face with someone and you forced a voice recorder in their face and said, 'What's your name?' You can imagine the response you would receive from the living; this is reflected in the spirit world also. Being aware of body language, the tone of your voice, and the emotion with which you ask the questions will, more often than not, yield results of greater clarity.

Making your connection is a real test of your people skills, your ability to be approachable, and your ability to understand your entity. However, this is where the definitions of entities can become murky. In time, researchers will begin to understand the need to identify whether they are dealing with a simple Intelligent Spirit or something else.

Experience is key and making sure you are dealing with a true spirit is vital for the safety of yourself, your team, and your clients. Being a bright light in a dark sky attracts flies. An old friend whom I trusted and continue to trust to this very day gave a word of warning to me a long time ago. He said, 'Don't burn too bright … or they see you.'

This brings us to the next definition of spirit.

Demonic/Inhuman:

Ah, the Inhuman, the Hollywood favorite aspect of the paranormal, the mere mention of which conjures up images of guys with little red horns and pitchforks. The reality of Inhuman entities, however, is truly nothing either to laugh at or take lightly.

The most dangerous type of a haunting you can run into is that of the Inhuman. The Inhuman differs from the other spirits you may encounter, as it is a spirit that has never been alive like you and me. Inhumans can be the worst of the worst in the spiritual realm and are often linked to demonic possession.

However, Inhumans also include more unconventional types of hauntings such as angelic interaction, which can be quite pleasant in contrast to the demonic interaction. Other types of Inhuman entities are known commonly as Incubus, Succubus, Elementals, Fairies, and Banshees, just to name a few. "Demon" is the term often used by some in the field to refer to the darker Inhuman entities. Other terms used to describe these are daemon, dæmon and daimon, which stem from different areas and time periods throughout European development, particularly Greece and Rome.

Inhumans are not tied to just one primary location or time period like the residual apparition. This freedom can make them very hard to pin down and to deal with.

So, how does a malevolent Inhuman spirit come to be in this earthly realm? How does it find ways to cause people distress, rip apart families and homes? How is it that some entities can even influence some victims to take their own lives?

Many theories have surfaced and circulated over the years. Of course, the Ouija board is among the most common and well known. However, it is very important to note that it truly is not the board itself that opens the doorway for an Inhuman spirit to enter. Simply the mental openness that is presented when someone takes parts in such things is what can lead to problems. Any dark rituals, séances, or Ouija board sessions can present a problem. Most often the people who are trying these things are teenagers, and most often they are ill prepared if something does come forth.

Even a seasoned investigator, regardless of age, can have a hard time with an Inhuman, as it is not something that can be easily controlled.

Still other theories exist. One being that these spirits have always been present upon the earth and are simply looking for humans that are in emotional or spiritual peril -- people that are easily tempted and controlled. Examples would be people in the middle of a spiritual crisis, a family situation, or simply an emotional downward spiral. These people are believed to be of a weaker mindset and therefore in theory are easier to influence.

Due to the often-tricky nature of the Inhuman presence, it is critical that you look for signs of what you may be dealing with. Examples include:

- Phantom scents of foul odors such as rotting flesh, feces, sulfa, or vomit.
- Small clouds of smoke, spontaneous fires and mild to severe temperature changes.
- Audible screams, growls, groans, wails, and loud bangs.

This subject is full of facts, incredibly detailed ones, many of them simply coming from each succeeding writer borrowing from his predecessors. Historians are very good at uncovering such things. Some of it was simply re-interpreting various beliefs of the pagans, heathens, and peasants within an inherited schema; most of it was simply made up. But new research into these entities is coming to light.

Every bookstore in America and around the world contains New Age books filled with remarkable stories of what spirits do and how to communicate with them. However, few mid-range books look at the darker side of the field and we have emphasized a greater concentration of information on this topic for you.

In this shady area of paranormal research we assume the invaders identity, as we have no solid facts about the identity of the entities, only those passed down from one era to the next. If there is anything we have learned from researching this darker level of the paranormal, it is that nothing is ever as it seems. Misdirection is always a tool used and this is why we have concentrated more so on the remedy rather than wasting valuable time on further identification.

Some forms of possession are felt and sensed during certain rituals by various religions and cults around the world. There is a difference in that these possessions are allowed to happen where as the others felt by the normal person on the street can endure for weeks and years as the possessing entity tries to get a hold first through oppression. There are similar signs within the initial onset of possession that mirror the experiences one would experience with Night Terrors (See Night Terrors for more) and the "old hag" phenomenon.

There may also be clues in the appearance of the dwelling itself. Unexplainable destruction of property may occur, such as holes in the wall, doors ripped from hinges, peeling of wallpaper, scratches in wood flooring, or furniture.

The occupants of the dwelling, as well as investigators, who are present, may experience unexplained feelings of depression, confusion, anger, and uncontrollable rage, even thoughts of suicide.

You should carefully study and interview clients and residents who may be part of a possible Inhuman case. Ask questions such as:

- Do you believe the spirit is dangerous or malevolent in nature?
- Has anyone in the house noted a change in their personality or that of another occupant?
- Has anyone there been to see a counselor for mood disorders, anger or depression?
- Do they feel stressed out or apathetic?

It has been reported that in a small percentage of Inhuman cases, the reported activity ceases when the afflicted attends counseling and even higher success rates with those who attend religious services.

Demonic possession has been well noted for a long time and made famous in many popular movies and television programs. In many cases the afflicted may not even realize that they are acting differently, though it will be noticeable to others.

Sometimes household pets may also pick up on the change in an individual. Animals that would once be very close with people in the home may suddenly shy away from the afflicted or be aggressive around them.

Early awareness and identification of an Inhuman case is imperative for safety and for an appropriate investigation. Without causing alarm, it should be discussed within the investigative team and for the time being, not brought to the attention of your client or clients. You do not want to alarm them until you are able to garner enough evidence to be sure of that with which you are dealing.

In this situation it is beneficial to have a teammate with you at all times during the investigation for safety reasons, as well as to keep each other's mental health in check.

Inhumans are noted for being very powerful and have been known to physically manipulate adults of all sizes and in some cases rendering them powerless. Of course, such events are extremely rare, but nonetheless possible.

A more common occurrence is fatigue of the physical and or mental kind. You may experience sudden feelings of dread and or nausea. It may appear difficult to draw a deep breath or to focus your vision. Once again the Inhuman entity is working on wearing you down, breaking you down systematically so that it may continue its path and plan for the inhabitant of the dwelling.

In forms of possession we can see a sharp inclination to shy away from healthy foods and to crave foods that ultimately are unhealthy for us and break down the body's defenses even more.

So how do you best approach a case that you think may be the activity of an Inhuman?

Try the following:

- Be in a good place mentally, spiritually, and physically.
- Avoid negativity at all costs -- push any negative thoughts from your mind, for throughout the case they will tend to grow.
- If you are a spiritual person and have a personal religious belief, pray as often as possible.

Removing an Inhuman spirit is not the easiest of tasks that a paranormal investigator faces.

Teaching your clients to empower themselves and to be assertive in their spaces is the primary step. You will often hear the phrase "Take back your own place." This can be done by strong vocalization and the removal of fear. Once you can do this, the Inhumans will usually seem to lose their hold and slip off to find an easier target.

For religious clients, blessings from clergy members often are very helpful. Holy water, Sage rubs, and various talismans are also effective depending upon the belief instilled in them.

Regardless of your personal beliefs and affiliations, be very wary and always on the alert when encountering something that never was of this world.

Night Terrors
Phenomenon and Defense

*The following information is a result of many years of research and should only be used as a guide. Any person wanting to adjust their diets and mineral intake should seek medical advice from their GP or medical practitioner first.

Much has been written and studied throughout history on Night Terrors, or Night Attacks. Though not necessarily a type of "ghost" per se, it is closely linked with much of what we have already discussed and thus warrants being presented.

Before we delve into this legitimate worldly phenomenon, we offer a few accounts from various people around the world and what they experienced:

> *"I was on lying on my back when I heard snuffling sounds; there was nothing that I saw, however I knew it was male. I felt an incredible weight on my chest, as if somebody put a large boulder there and somebody had their hand against my throat. I was terrified."*

> *"When the 'visitor' returns I have always been rendered helpless until the 'assailant' has finished doing whatever it is that they paralyze me for."*

> *"Nothing can convince me that I imagined what happened to me. The other night's experience was the most terrifying yet because I actually fought it off me at one point and managed to break the paralyzing 'spell' it first puts your body in a state of, I was fighting my way out from under it."*

"I want to learn what it actually is, what the motives are behind the attack. I find this hard to explain but they try to make you forget it happened, or forget certain details that confirm to you that this thing did happen and couldn't have been a dream. The other night was the first time I have been able to remember certain details that confirm that this happened and there WAS something else in the room with me."

Night terrors have been happening to man for thousands of years, yet in western society we still know little about them apart from the medical aspect, which we will deal with a little later.

These attacks were believed to be instigated by spirits or demons. A number of Middle Eastern and European texts have described in some part the first impressions of the attacks, such as leaping upon, crushing, and oppressing individuals as they attempt to sleep at night. Throughout the ages these attacks have been listed in various forms such as the Greek Mora, the Roman Incubus, German mar, Czech murea, Polish zmora, Russian kikimora and the French cauchmar.

More recently all the definitions have come under one heading from Newfoundland known as Ag Rog, or the 'Old Hag'. It was believed that the incubi were to be found in the remote areas of the desert and would take on various forms during these attacks and sometimes were not seen at all. The Latin verb incubare, the derivative of 'incubus,' is basically translated into 'to lie upon.' It's remarkable to see, no matter the social background of the victims -- whether they are based in western culture or the remotest part of Africa -- the attacks all bear a remarkable similarity that is not affected by social upbringing.

However modern psychiatry does not consider demonic possession to be a clinical reality and from some perspectives we can understand, as there is no real scientific, tangible proof of demons.

But more enlightened practitioners and researchers acknowledge that something outside the body may have the ability to influence the human mind. They now feel that certain types of psychoses such as schizophrenia, or any sudden or radical change in behavior, could indicate the signs of a possession from whatever source may have invaded or controls the host's body. These new beliefs have come from hours of observation and recording.

In the worst-case scenario we can see the possession having a detrimental effect on the victim's life. The possession can reach climax where the person may commit a heinous, violent crime or exhibit anti-social behavior and even a self-destructive path that ultimately leads to suicide.

Recent research has shown that the onset of depression, which affects 50% more women than men, can in some instances lead to those individuals hearing voices trying to get them to commit suicide. Hormone Treatment Therapy, it was suggested by one person, can stop the voices (HRT) as described by one such victim of these silent voices, but we have not been able to confirm this.

The Christian Church believes that one of the signs of possession is the ability to speak in tongues and perform lewd acts whilst avoiding religious artifacts such as the crucifix and rosary, but we believe the actual artifact itself possess no power. It's what it represents and that's not the humanization of the religion but rather the goodness and truth, which are the building blocks of all the major religions. It's the humanization of these basic truths that have lead to a breakdown and the subsequent fracturing to form the various religions seen around the world today. According to one clinical psychologist and the late Catholic Exorcist Father Malachi Martin, over 50% of those confined in mental hospitals in the United States are not insane but rather victims of some form of possession from unknown sources.

Many believe that harmony and balance in your own mind, body, and spirit is necessary to place a barrier against these attacks. Certainly we have discovered over the course of our investigations into the night terror attacks that a healthy diet is vital in stopping these attacks, which will be explained in a short time. But first, it's prudent to acknowledge that there are medical factors that can also produce effects similar to that experienced by those which fall under Night Attacks. Narcolepsy is a disabling illness that affects on average 1 in 2,000 people. Most of the individuals with the disorder are not diagnosed and, thus, sadly, are not treated. The disease is principally characterized by a permanent and overwhelming feeling of sleepiness and fatigue.

Abnormalities in rapid eye movement (REM) sleep can led to sufferers experiencing a cycle time of 60 minutes in REM rather than the healthier 90 minutes which over the course of time can produce dream-like hallucinations and finding oneself physically weak or paralyzed for a few seconds upon waking. Narcolepsy is a frequent disorder, the second leading cause of excessive daytime sleepiness, but let's not forget nighttime attacks can produce the same exhaustion from a sever attack as those predisposed to suffer from Narcolepsy.

During REM the brain becomes very active in the alpha cycle range. Dreams are somewhat triggered by pons which are located in the base of the brain. Signals from these are sent to the thalamus, which relay them to the cortex that also shut off the neurons in the spinal cord, and this causes the temporary paralysis of the body. This is so we do not act out our dreams. Sometimes this process doesn't quite work as we can see from those individuals that sleep walk and sometimes act out their dreams in a somewhat clumsy fashion.

Since the 1960's it has been known that several disabling symptoms of narcolepsy such as sleep paralysis and hypnologic hallucinations were simply pathological equivalents of REM sleep. During sleep paralysis the patients suddenly finds themselves unable to move for a few minutes, most often upon falling asleep or waking up. The sufferers experience dream like auditory or visual hallucinations usually whilst dozing and falling asleep. If we don't see it, we class it as a hallucination, but how do we know? We already have shown that things happen outside of the visual and auditory ranges of the conscious human, does the paranormal community need to go back and look at this again with a wider viewpoint?

One would be quick to back the medical examination of night terrors and in many cases would be quite right to do so. However there are a few discrepancies, which don't appear to have happened in the sleep labs, which allow us the ability to differentiate between narcolepsy and the true night terror.

During most night terror attacks the victims are in deep sleep or have not yet entered sleep. They are woken or attracted by a movement that has entered the room. Even those in deep sleep are woken to a strange and unsettling atmosphere. Most will hear footsteps move closer and or either feel a weight on the bed and as the accounts at the beginning tell us they feel a weight on their chest and a tightening of the throat. We believe these entities are gaining energy from the core, the heart of the body. During some instances, people being pulled onto their backs and exposing their power centers has allowed this phenomenon to continue. Sleeping on their stomachs stops this event from occurring.

One particular account stated that most people being attacked on a psychical level were mentally ill -- one which we thought was quite a harsh line from someone who would be better off researching the subject a little better before commenting. However, he goes on to explain that to hear voices tormenting or commanding them to commit anti-social acts may suffer from hallucinations and think they are being assaulted. But in tests we discovered disembodies voices that were shown to have effects on mediums whilst sitting in circle. As the medium tried to make contact with these entities, we actually recorded the words being whispered before the medium spoke the same word and received their impression. The singular words were being whispered at a rate much higher than that, which could be produced by the human voice and indicates that something out there could influence what we think.

Further tests are being designed to witness if selections of people are able to hear either consciously or unconsciously within these regions. With the shocking evidence so far we are no nearer the truth of life after death, but we are confident there is something more outside the body which we clearly heard influencing someone's perceptions. The bigger question is, how many thoughts during the day actually belong to us and are not whispered from a distant place not that far away? We're not that quick anymore to write criminals off who said they were influenced by voices to commit their crime. However, we still believe they do have free will and they acted to cause the crime and should still pay for their misdeeds, but we understand the mental strain they may have been under to act.

So how can one help prevent these forms of attack from happening? It seems the evidence points toward a dietary problem. Insufficiencies in diet may lead to an increase in attacks and possible possession. Most of these attacks can happen between 3 and 5 a.m. Sometimes victims may be lucky that it only happens once in their lifetime; others may be less fortunate as attacks can happen nightly.

If we look at the old belief systems and their superstitions, we can see in Europe for instance followers of magic used a piece of iron to deflect negativity. It was commonly believed iron stopped the flow of psychic energy and was used when one felt emotionally wrought or under some form of psychic attack for instance the evil eye. Iron was inscribed with symbolic Mars and worn as a protective defense against negative magic. It was customary to take iron nails and insert them in white or blue candles for protection. It was alleged to have the dubious ability to break spells since antiquity.

An old Pennsylvanian Dutch charm against the evil eye and negativity asked you to wear an old iron safety pin in the sleeve or your shirt. It was alleged that if iron was used in conjunction with copper it maintained a balance with the energies and chemistry of the body. Iron already exists naturally in the body; it is also used in the treatment of various blood disorders, muscular atrophy, sore throat, gall and kidney stones, and some forms of internal bleeding.

Both the reproductive system and our fingernails and toenails already benefit from a healthy intake of iron.

All the views of the attacks given by the victims may have reflected a dietary deficiency or possible anemia, which may have allowed the door to open for these attacks to happen. So for those that suffered the attacks we began to ask the question in regards to their diet and around 70% of the cases indicated a lack in iron rich food. Iron deficiency, anemia, often attacks pre-menopausal women, who would regularly take nonsteroidial, anti-inflammatory drugs. A vast majority of the attacks occur in those that have not reached the menopause.

But women were not the only victims for attacks. A small minority of men also suffered from the night terrors. Although men suffer less from iron deficiency, it does happen. But once again if we set aside the medical causes of iron deficiency it still calls into question the modern life style and our requirement for a quick fix in regards to our diet. We rarely sit down to a complete meal because of any number of factors such as not enough time or to great an expense. In regards to the costs of eating healthy we believe this is why we see a higher rate of night terror attacks than those more financially better off, who have the time and wealth to eat healthier.

But with only a slight change in our diet we can increase the iron and vitamins such as B12 to balance out immune system to fight off the attacks naturally. We should certainly consider eating red meat or iron rich vegetables. Darker cut meats usually indicate a richer iron base, but vegetarians may want to try legumes, fortified cereals, quinoa, kale and other green leafy vegetables. It's a good idea to top these foods with a rich source of vitamin C, like lemon juice. The vitamin C will help the body absorb the iron. We do advise, should you feel like these factors apply to you, consult your doctor about a healthier diet and have tests run on your iron levels.

Following an attack, victims report slipping into a mild depression and over sustained periods of attack they obviously fall deeper into that awful pit. This can be countered with omega three fatty acids -- the essential fats found in seafood. You can either keep your brain running smoothly or clog it up with the wrong types of fat.

As in forms of possession, with night attacks we often see a sharp inclination to shy away from healthy foods and to crave foods that ultimately are unhealthy for us and break down the body's defenses even more. Omega three fatty acids play a major role in brain function. They even boost your mood but although the body requires the fat acids of omega three, we cannot make it on our own. Essential fatty acids only appear through your diet.

New medical evidence suggests the omega three fatty acids found in fish called docosahexaenoic acid (DHA) and eicosapentaenoic (EPA) can help drive away depression. Along with omega three you may also wish to consider a sweet potato or a spinach salad. Both are rich in folate acid and vitamin B6 or pyridoxine. Deficiencies in these two vitamins can also bring on depression. Vitamin B6 works by keeping the brains neurotransmitters in balance. Other sources of this vitamin can be found in navy beans and bananas. Sticking with whole wheat breads and watermelons can also help spike your thiamine levels helping you feel more clear headed and energetic.

As in all aspects of the paranormal field and life in general, a healthy balance between mind, spirit and body is beneficial to handle whatever comes your way.

Chapter 2

Is There Anybody Out There?

Understanding the Metaphysical Realm

*"What lies behind us and what lies before us
are tiny matters compared to what lies within us."*

RALPH WALDO EMERSON

Just because we cannot see it, doesn't mean it's not there.

If anything, the recently introduced 'Full Spectrum Camera' to the research field has shown that indeed there are things happening around us that we humans cannot see. On some level some of us can sense it -- the skin has an ability to pick out information from the environment and send information to the brain for processing that we simply cannot understand (later in this publication, we will address some experiments being conducted in this area).

Scientists once believed that humans had the best eyesight in the animal kingdom; as it turned out, we have one of the worst, and many animals surpass our abilities, both in sight, smell, touch, and hearing. Furthermore, these animals can react to an environment that we call haunted.

Why? What do they sense that we cannot?

Finding answers to these questions -- this is why we must continue to work hard on breaking down this wall of ignorance, and I pray it's a wall that, once down and we see what is behind it, we can put back up if required (we should not forget the fable of Pandora's box).

This ... is where metaphysics comes into play. But as with nearly every new scientific introduction, skeptics abound.

Metaphysics, or the new science, has come under some harsh scientific spotlights, which has stripped away the outer layers to reveal a center where nothing exists. In other words it has revealed the metaphysical underworld to be nothing more than words. Nothing is left for scientific analysis. As it cannot be measured in a lab or scrutinized under a microscope, in modern scientific standards, it is nothing more than simply myth, an old wives tale told by fanciful minds and wishful thinkers around a campfire.

But ...

We tend to forget that yesterday; science was seen as the 'end all' to every question, yet as time has passed, those theories of old (which, we might add, were said to be set in concrete) seemed to fall apart at the seams. Science as we know it is not an exact truth; it, too, has to evolve. As time changes with new discoveries, so, too, does science.

Metaphysics lingers in a world of quantum mechanics that until recently no one even considered seriously. Physicists will openly talk about the possibility of worlds existing in parallel universes, while those that mention they have fairies at the bottom of the garden are seen as needing some help, maybe a pill or two. Yet this has been recognized in the metaphysical world for hundreds of years. Even today, though under a new name, modern science frowns on it.

Druids were believed, by some, to have used portals, where, if entered at certain times of the year, they could see into another world -- one where the creatures are very different from ours. For brief moments in time both beings saw each other and, on occasion, information was exchanged. Or so the legends go.

Of course sometimes things just didn't go as planned. Across the globe, legends told of people begin taken by these creatures and returning sometime later, or even not returning at all. Research in Russia indicated that there might be seven different types of human, all on different paths, each not knowing about the other until something happens, and in those moments both beings see each other.

The Irish Druids where not the only ones to have access to these portals; it is believed they exist around the world. On one recent trip, we visited the biggest portal in the world, located in Brazil. Thankfully we remained alone during our visit. But usually the native culture is aware of these locations and we found it useful to exchange information.

Metaphysics in principle does seem to have some form of law, which must be followed, such as the Manifestation Scale we have been developing after years of observing the field and eyewitness accounts. But this is only a small piece of the pie and further work is required, though in part it has allowed us to develop a fix for some people that are plagued by the negative effects of hauntings.

How does it work?

Some sensitizes, people who claim to feel different energies but cannot determine information from it, mediums, psychics, some children and animals have all show unusual abilities to interact with this mysterious world.

What is it that they possess that the normal person does not? A lot of people who are not connected to this mysterious force are good at material business, situations in which the here-and-now applies. They are able to center their abilities to work on material issues and are very different individuals than those who have a connection with earth.

What may be the reason for this? Is there anyway that the ability could be enhanced for those individuals that wanted to?

Barry tells the following story:

I was working with a good friend of mind in USA about this very subject. Although he comes from a scientific background and was well versed in neuroscience, the science of the mind, we worked quiet well together. Of course, from time to time, we don't see eye to eye on theories, but for the most part, both of us were heading in the same direction.

From the work we did, there seemed to be a chemical effect that promoted psychic abilities and others that would lessen their effects.

A majority of this seemed to depend on our diet. Of course we cannot say for sure, but the research seemed to indicate that this might indeed be the case. Age was another factor. Biological development within the body on a majority of cases seemed to suggest that as our eyes developed they where becoming less able to see into particular light spectrums than those of our children.

The eyes are a funny old piece of equipment. We never really give them much credit and we can take a lot of their abilities for granted. Just take a moment to consider this: as you read these words you see the words and you assume you see them through your eyes.

Wrong. The eyes are hot-wired to the rear of the brain. The images are processed here, not at the front with the eyes. The information, when it reaches the brain, is actually upside down and the brain does a wonderful process of rectifying the images and we continue to go about our daily lives unaware what is actually happening.

And there's more. As our eyes develop as young children we begin to piece things together and we see the world with a different viewpoint than those of our parents. Approximately between the ages of three and seven, it has been suggested a filter develops over the eye and we can no longer see things that as developing children we used to see. The filter blocks out the UV light that can be harmful.

Consider what our kids tell us during those ages: some see people coming out from the wardrobe, or from under the bed, or even out from the closet. Yet we as adults, when we look, cannot see what our children have described. Yes over-active imaginations can be at fault, but on many occasions there is much more to consider. They are able to put more detail into the described image and sometimes their fear can tell us a lot.

If the entity is seen on more than one occasion then we can obtain a better description. The full spectrum camera taps into some of that area that we as adults lack. The camera has been designed to capture light from 1100nm (nanometers, the unit of light measurement) in the infrared range through visible light that we can see and into the ultra-violet range of 300nm. It is speculated that some adults may still be able to see partially into these ranges.

It's very interesting that the UV range is the higher energy, and mediums and psychics for years were shouting from the roof tops that these entities were in a higher energy and had to slow down to materialize in this plane of existence. It seems that science and metaphysics may have met in the middle here as we begin to see that there is more activity in the UV bands than the IR. But you may find that the more aware the entity is, the trickier it can be to the capture an image of it.

We have been working for many years observing the materialization scale and understand a particular process must occur for spirits to appear in the here-and-now. If they choose, they can observe us whilst outside this process and no matter what piece of equipment we use we will not be able to reach them. The spirits can simply stay behind the veil of shadow. During the materialization the spirit will become susceptible to our laws of psychics and this is where we can capture their progress.

Spirits can linger at stage 1 of the materialization scale and simply influence our thoughts or, in some cases, guide us in our day-to-day lives. But even here, should the influence be negative, we have developed a process where we can give back balance to the individual and alleviate the symptoms should the individual become at risk to themselves or others. Our own body has an immune system that is our first line of defense and particular minerals can boost this wall, as it will inevitably become damaged form a negative influence.

The manifestation scale will continue to the point of materialization some steps later, and it is here that we can see the entity in full form, either as solid, sometimes a white mist or black shadow. The majority of spirit manifestation will occur at night, when reduced UV aids the final stages. This is why it's important to shoot the full spectrum to be able to capture the UV ranges without having to produce UV in the environment, as it will most certainly make the entity reverse the process and flee the scene.

Some researchers, including us, for now will follow the theory that as the spirit develops, the atoms used to form itself will become excited by the UV in natural or man-made lights.

For instance, UV is naturally in the atmosphere even at night due in part to the shape of the atmosphere. It will loop around, obviously nowhere near as much as daylight, but add the effect of the moon where direct sunlight from the moon's surface is reflected to the earth's surface and a higher level of UV will become present. As the particles in the atom become excited, they will vibrate. Each particle in each atom reaches a point of excitement and is expelled through the roof of the atom, becoming fluorescent. But strong UV will break down these bonds and the materialization will fall apart.

We have been in sittings with mediums where darker entities will try and gain control of the subject. Once the strong UV is introduced, on the sound recordings you hear their pleas to turn off the light. It has become a safeguard and only used as a last resort.

Tap into it?

Metaphysics is split into many different areas that would be impossible to research individually in a lifetime. But we have tried to cover as much ground as possible.

Tapping into the shadow realms can be difficult but over time it can happen. Patience is a virtue not awarded to man though so we have a few recommendations that will quicken your steps.

'Bio-feedback' is a process in which we can observe the chemical reaction in our skin.

A series of experiments is being conducted in the USA and early results have indicated some wonderful possibilities. A series of pictures, randomized by a computer, is displayed via a screen to the subject, who is connected to a biofeedback monitor. We can see that as the images continue to remain pleasant, the chemical reaction in the skin is calm and low.

But when the computer selects a disturbing image, the chemical reaction will sharply increase.

What has this to do with Metaphysics?

It seems that during this process of randomization of the pictures, the skin is reacting milliseconds before the picture is displayed. In part we are reacting to something that has not yet happened. You may have heard similar accounts from tales of people traveling along a road and suddenly they slow down before an obstacle appears that would have for sure killed them. It seems the biggest organ our bodies possess, the skin, has an ability to tap information from the environment around us and feed it -- like our eyes -- back to the brain where it is processed in record time and we act. Or on many occasions don't and regret not listening to that voice inside our head.

Many people believe it was angels or guides that reached to them. We cannot dispute that, as we cannot prove otherwise. But for now we understand we can tap into a universal system of information and use this and many of us do it as a daily process and never know it. Just think the next time you drive your vehicle along a dark road -- your headlights allow you to see up to 30 feet of clear vision and yet we travel at 70 mph, well above the ability to stop in that distance should an obstacle be in our way. Why? How? Maybe we are tapping into more than we know.

From what we can gather, the majority of psychics get a lot of information in quiet times and especially in the time between consciousness and sleep -- this netherworld of shadow and illusion, not knowing what is real and what isn't. But those that have gained the ability to hold that brain pattern as long as they can have turned out to be very good psychics.

So what is happening here? The brain is caught between two brain patterns; a conscious mind fights with its subconscious mind, both demanding attention, both possessing explosive capabilities. This process can be duplicated and enhanced by our dietary intake, foods such as pasta, bread, and potatoes will greatly restrict the forming of melatonin, whereas chicken and turkey will promote its development and will cause the person to become drowsy. This is where you must gain control of the fighting brain. Some would argue it's seratonin and others melatonin, but for now it's still up for debate. Either way, the production of these chemicals in the brain can promote psychic ability and like the aforementioned food types can hinder it and slow it to a stop.

One famous scientist, Friedrick Kekule, was dogmatic about finding the molecular structure of benzene. It was giving him great trouble and he could not get that break, but one night as he simply rested by his open fire and hovered in the area between sleep and wakefulness, his mind gave him the vision of a snake eating its own tail forming what was recognized as a circle. His conscious mind kicked into gear and lifted him from his restful peace and he realized the answer was presented to him as he identified that benzene was a closed carbon ring that revolutionized modern chemistry.

During his presentation to a gathering of scientists and scholars, he concluded with, "Let us dream, gentlemen, and then we may perhaps find the truth."

Finding evidence of the metaphysical world in your day-to-day life

Finding the old world will take us to leave our office blocks and concrete cities. We need to make a reconnection with the earth. By this we don't mean to become hippies or anything like that, but we as a human race have become more distant from our earth unlike any other animal in existence.

Before we developed electricity we began down a road of industrial revolution, which led to some wonderful developments, inventions, and medicines that would save thousands of lives, but we also invented machines and weapons that killed millions. We, like no other animal on earth, are capable of such bloodshed, the ability to strip the earth and move on like a plague, leaving the ground and air ravished.

Seers and prophets in Celtic lore were able to look ahead for a week at a time and determine the weather and when the best time was to plant. We're aware of native people in Peru that can tell their farmers where to plant for the best food and where it will not be affected by weather. In the animal kingdom, horses will stand with their backs to the trees as a storm front approaches and we cannot see any clue of change; some cows will sit down when the rain approaches and stand again as its about to pass. Yet modern man -- even with satellite imagery -- sometimes cannot tell what the weather is going to do a few hours ahead, never mind a week ahead. We have lost touch with earth and some would even venture that we have lost the ability to hear God.

I would urge readers to take time and walk in a forest, mountains or the plains and turn off their modern take on the world which is vital, taking time for themselves and take time to listen. When was the last time you:

- Heard a bird sing?
- Smelt fresh pine?
- Witnessed a rainbow?
- Heard the earth?

Many of us who had Celtic ancestors may not be aware that they were very tuned into the earth in more ways than we could imagine. Previous archaeo-acoustic investigations of prehistoric, megalithic structures in England and Ireland have identified acoustic resonance at frequencies of 95–120 Hz, particularly near 110–120Hz, and all representing pitches in the human vocal range.

These locations severed as spiritual centres where Neolithic man could communicate with their gods with the aid of ritual chanting. Activity in the left temporal region of the human brain was found to be significantly lower at 110 Hz than at other frequencies. Additionally, the pattern of asymmetric activity over the prefrontal cortex shifted from one of higher activity on the left at most frequencies to right sided dominance at 110 Hz. These findings are compatible with relative deactivation of language centers and a shift in prefrontal activity that may be related to emotional processing or psychic reasoning.

They may have truly had a connection that we have subsequently lost.

Chapter 3

Who to Work With

Forming or Joining a Team

"*The important thing is this: to be able at any moment to sacrifice what we are for what we could become.*"

CHARLES DUBOIS

This field can be very useful in making new links and contacts that can, if addressed properly, last for years. Great friendships can develop, but if the challenges of the paranormal are not addressed, these links will be torn apart and can breakdown faster than you ever thought possible.

For this reason I prefer smaller groups of up to five people. Anymore than this and weaknesses within individuals' characters and such can and will be exploited and team dynamics '**WILL**' crumble in flames like the Hindenburg blimp. Remember to communicate with team members, as this is vital.

Making contact with like-minded people is much easier in today's society due to the use of the Internet and social networking websites that we all love or hate. But if used properly and with the right level of scrutiny, you can find and develop friends in this area from all over the world. Networking is extremely important to us, as we travel frequently and when we do, we try and meet groups from those countries and share research and make good friends as we go along.

The media love a good ghost story, especially around Halloween. If you approach the local press, you could swing an article about your ghost-hunting pastime and attract like-minded folks from your area. This is a good way to build your team numbers.

But a word of warning: The local press loves a good story and may add or remove details to support their needs. So, be careful and use the local media as much as they will use you, but don't depend on them. They should not become the group's crutch. Once you get yourselves established, keep a little distance.

Placing an ad in your local press will help attract attention to your group as well. This may be a cheaper option should you want to set up a team in your area. Money is often tight when you are beginning, so keeping costs low is one of the group's vital keys to success. Once you have come together and established a solid group, it may be an option for the team to take a fortnightly small collection of a few bucks from each member that will support new equipment and travel costs.

Over the course of a few months it's amazing how much the team can save. Different states and countries will have varying tax regulations, so it's best to check the group set-up with your local authorities, who will give you clearance to set up an official team bank account and have things all above board.

Why you shouldn't work alone?

What we cannot see cannot harm us … well, that's not quite true.

Working alone has its physical dangers. Like anything we do in daily life, there will be risks, but in this particular field there will be dangers which you cannot see which have been recognized in the metaphysical field for thousands of years. Yet today, we have become used to modern amenities.

However, the dangers to your entire person are more focused in this field than a lot of others, and can affect people extremely subtly and insidiously and, as previously mentioned, can break down friendships and families. A pattern is always in place and recognizing this pattern can help early detection of oppression. No doubt when people read this some will roll their eyes, but we are at greater threat from this than any other time in our modern history as we have some of our religious leaders commenting that there is no such evil as this.

A growing underground within the faiths is starting to address this, but unless we take charge of our own immediate safety we may be unlucky enough to experience one of these encounters that will ruin you and those around you.

(Our work on this subject will be written about in great detail in a companion publication called 'The Influence,' which gives readers the ability to see those clues and make necessary changes to address the physical changes and the mental issues that could occur.)

Practice, Practice, Practice: Learning the Ropes

1. How to use your equipment.

The technology used in the Paranormal community is changing faster than we can adapt, but one thing we're seeing is that there is much which simply does the same as the last -- it's just packaged differently. This is a great concern as it can lead serious investigations astray. (We've seen devices used to measure EMF that are not sensitive at all. That may be OK if you are haunted by an old washing machine or possessed TV, but that is about it.)

One piece of equipment is never useful. During an investigation, it's best to use two or three other pieces, which will support each other. Know where you are setting your equipment and of course be aware of the direction toward which it is capable of recording. A lot of the modern EVP devices such as the very reliable Zoom H2 are exceptional at recording broadcast quality sounds and out-strips the other cheaper recorders on the market. With the ability to change out SD cards during your investigation and easy file transfer to computers for analysis, this product is second to none.

Others on the market have directional microphones with drops in signal near the center of twin microphones, but the H2 has four on-board microphones giving a good 4-band 360-degree recording. This allows you to see on the appropriate computer software which direction the EVP was coming from inside your target area.

Of course there is a school of thought (of which we are supporters) that the microphones are being manipulated by a low level ELF, the type we are seeing with the natural EMF meter, with small fluctuations in the DC magnetic and electrical ranges.

Equipment such as the Paranormal Puck by Digital Dowsing can home in on these with some strong eyebrow-raising results if stimulated by the DC fields. Even though the Puck has been controversial, it is worth taking a look at. The software package can really help the researchers see the stimulus and corresponding results.

Another piece of equipment is called the EMF listener -- a device that takes those low-end ELF and gives them a voice so that you can hear them in a room. The device is very sensitive and can pick up on signals that the majority of paranormal teams don't have the capabilities to record. Both companies have been very reasonable and their equipment warrants serious investigation by dedicated teams.

2. Troubleshooting malfunctioning equipment.

This can be very troubling. Getting the right case to protect your equipment is vital. Prevention is better than cure. For bigger teams with a wider budget you may wish to look at Pelican Cases, a versatile case made from hard plastic and can be filled with foam for all manner of equipment. They are not cheap but will last for decades and come complete with locks and air stabilization for air travel. It also floats, though we hope never to witness it in action.

For the most part, teams will stay to their own areas, so moderate packaging will do just as well. But after every third investigation you should clean everything with a fine brush and evaporating cleaner. This will remove any dirt particles, which can be troublesome to electronics and cameras. If the team can afford the change, rechargeable batteries (1200nhm or higher) should be used and should be completely used before recharging, as this will extend the life of the batteries. Some chargers don't switch off and will overcharge, so watch out for this when you make your purchase.

If you have an official piece of equipment that is malfunctioning, have a specialist look into it and have it repaired. A specialist, for example, should calibrate thermal cameras, once a year. This will help you understand your results and know that your camera is performing within its specified design capabilities.

3. Common pitfalls.

A common pitfall is not knowing your equipment. Some people jump straight into it and decide the evidence they collected must be proof of the paranormal without understanding their devices or their limitations.

One example is orbs, perfect circles captured on digital cameras. These are a thorn in the side of the paranormal investigator and can lead to heated debates. Some are convinced they are signs of spirit activity, but they are simply dust or water particles. Others will claim that there was no dust in the air, but there is always dust in the air. Our skin sheds itself one piece at a time, making up 60% of dust in our homes. These are caught in the air current and as the dust particle is lit in the flash, the focus of the camera is unable to adjust to the spec of dust and the particle is exposed as a round ball of light (which some say have faces inside and such).

Place a camera on a tripod, turn off the flash, take your shots, and see how many dust orbs you find in your shot. Then repeat the process with the flash on.

4. Knowing what to look for.

There are hundreds of books out there in the new age bookshelves telling you what to look out for, but really it's about experience and talking. If you have problem and would like an answer, talk to someone who has been in the field for a time. Ask them their opinion and learn from their knowledge and grow on that. Don't rest on every word -- develop and grow your own knowledge base and then share it with those coming behind you.

A certain amount of knowledge is good going into paranormal research and can be gained from such books as

'Psychic Self Defense' by Dion Fortune. 'When the ghost screams' by Leslie Rule was another wonderful book.

Keep in mind, some things you read will not sit well with you, but take on board what does and apply it to your work. If it works then you have a break through, if it doesn't don't hold your head and feel sorry for yourself. Get up and try another, and another, and another until it does work.

5. Changing plans and taking cues from the case.

This is where experience really comes into it. Like most detectives, after a while, you get a feel for the case. Certain hunches can lead to many breakthroughs. It's like being a paranormal profiler -- you have to get into the spirits heads and know who they were, what they did, their aspirations, their hates, and work your way into their world. Psychics do this often to a certain degree, but the good profiler will find them.

Many are frightened and should be treated with compassion and understanding as such. Many who are angry hide so they will not be found. Previous sites that have been active will suddenly go still once you introduce a voice recorder to it so its true identity will not be uncovered. A rigid team will not develop and cannot hope to advance the field if they do not bend to the stimulus of the wind and many will fall by the wayside.

6. Where to practice -- grave stomping, respect and legal issues.

We rarely, if ever, investigate graveyards. That's like fishing in a small pond filled with gold fish -- you are sure of a hit. It's easy and it should never be easy. What do you hope to gain by investigating a place that will not challenge you to grow and learn?

Respect and legal issues have always been a problem for some teams, and we, too, have climbed that wall to gain access to a site we should not have been in. But in the growing society of security and threats, it's best to keep to the legal route. Get permission first, even if it takes a long time. Keep at it and be persistent.

Chapter 4

Know Your Gear

Equipment Overview

"The illiterate of the 21st century will not be those who cannot read and write, but those who cannot learn, unlearn, and relearn."

ALVIN TOFFLER

What to use

We are moving into an area where new technology is coming into the field of paranormal research. Around the world, serious research teams have been silently testing new equipment, designed, like most in science, from observation. New cameras are now available from a company based in the USA. Built by engineers, the new technology is producing DVR/USB cameras which simply plug and play and can look into higher areas of the UV spectrum which were previously undetectable. Mediums often claim that some spirits are of a higher energy and they have to slow down in order to communicate with us here in this 'Earth plane.' Interestingly the UV is the higher energy and we are beginning to see some really strange things appear in our cameras.

Where to use it, where not to use it

This can test the team greatly, leading it to think both inside and outside the box. Understanding your environment and stimuli created there to create a bridge between spirit and this reality needs to be considered. But first, some groundwork is required.

Yes, marching into an area blind can yield results, but without doing your homework beforehand you may discover it is nothing more than contamination from man-made devices or natural phenomenon which you would have discovered in a pre-tour of the location.

Keep a small pocket notebook and pen handy. If you heard anything you can identify at the time, note it and the camera's time code so you will not be fooled when you are trawling through your analysis. Once again this reflects back on your equipment in that you keep it time coded to your own timepiece. It makes it much easier to correlate information from multiple devices and cross-referencing with your notebook.

If you are going to an environment with high levels of EMF (Electro Magnetic Fields) you may wish to limit your time there. Research from Europe has suggested that pulsed EMF can trigger hallucinations that will fall into the categories of sight, hearing, touch, and even smell. So having the proper EMF reader -- one whose sensitivity you can adjust -- would be essential in that type of situation. However, spirits manipulate the low end EMF or more commonly known ELF (Extra Low Frequency), and we should not forget the amazing work conducted by John Hutchison, a Canadian researcher who has shown some amazing results in high end EMF.

In his lab, Hutchinson has had continual results introducing high levels of EMF to various objects, which then change and then don't behave, as they should. For example, metal rods will be destroyed at the molecular level, twisted and deformed and non-magnetic objects such as wood and plastic will suddenly react to these fields. One experiment is said to have taken a metal rod, held down on a table by two wooden strips, which were securely screwed down.

The rod was then introduced to the EMF and heated to an extent where the rod turned white. Tremendous heat was generated and yet when the experiment was concluded the two wooden straps were not even burned. How on earth could this happen?

In other tests, objects such as a bowling ball would levitate in the lab; countless objects would be fired around a room for no reason as if thrown by an invisible hand; mysterious fires would start in concrete some distance from the machines (concrete does not burn easily -- the temperatures required are extremely high).

Two things would spring to the mind of the seasoned investigator at this point: 1) could these high level EMFs be responsible for poltergeist phenomenon, and 2) the fires in the concrete have a stark resemblance to spontaneous human combustion (SHC). Claims of SHC have stated the heat would have been tremendous inside the body to burn part of it to powder. Likewise the heat needed to burn concrete is equally high, but SHC causes no other damage around. One eyewitness account from a fire department in the USA claimed the victim of such a phenomenon was lying on the stairs as the firemen entered, a small blue flame was emanating from the victim's stomach and as soon as they put their water on to him he was engulfed in flames. It was suggested the heat might have been so intense that the water was split into hydrogen and oxygen, causing the victim to ignite in a fireball. Effectively the very act of attempting to save this individual may have indeed accelerated his death.

Hutchison witnessed something even stranger. The high levels of EMF could remain high for weeks in the lab with nothing happening, until someone walked inside. For some bizarre reason we are becoming a trigger for this phenomenon on the higher sides of the EMF within the lab, possibly reflecting back onto the poltergeist phenomenon.

Why you should use it and how to use it

For a long time metaphysics has relied heavily on the medium and sensitives. For those on the other side of the coin, equipment was the only course to at least try and understand this area of research. To a point it still is the same way, but with more equipment becoming available to the developing teams we are beginning to see another revolution occur.

Continual research has led to the development of new equipment that is helping us explore areas that previously where only suggested by the mediums. Places that we could not see, yet some of those sensitives could, and because we could not see them or hear them we claimed they did not exist. That's no longer the case. We are beginning to witness those things now also, but it took us nearly a century to catch up. Maybe the world is finally ready to make a jump in this field of research.

Those who read books or watch TV documentaries about these subjects will think even more now when the new research starts to hit the world stage, challenging those that remained in the 'no' camp to re-think their status and shake up their world.

You may be aware turtles are slow, but they also see slowly. For instance, they would be only slightly aware of children playing close by. The turtle's brain processes the images slower than those processed by human brains. We simply move faster than the turtle can see. Is it possible ghosts or energy beings are simply moving faster then we can see?

When an image strikes our retina the nerve impulses last approximately 1/25 sec. For this reason motion pictures appear to move continuously, even though the number of frames/sec. is not extremely fast. If you have seen some "old time movies" from the 1920s and '30s, they appear "jerky" because at the time the technology did not allow for frames to appear quickly enough to "fool" the eye, and the eye was able to see successive frames.

Here in rests a problem though. We can incorporate a high-resolution camera to capture 120/250 frames per second, but for it to work properly requires more light. The more lightly we apply the less likely we are to see manifestation. This is a problem we are working hard to try and rectify, but in the meantime we have to deal with the slower frame rate and isolate the best light spectrum and also which area within that light spectrum would garner the best results.

What's the best tool for the job - (see Knowing Your Ghosts)

Listen to yourself -- this is the best tool in the case. You can go much further than your equipment but we still need to document the experiences and that's where the better technology comes into play. There was always voluptuous {Note from Erik: this word is out of context here … perhaps you meant something else?} claims from the sensitives that they could sense the spirit, and of course if all else failed, fall back onto their third eye and various chakras {Note from Erik: what are third eyes and chakras? Might need explaining}.

But as we wipe away our scientific smirk, in part they were right. It seems in recent trails in the lab that the biggest organ in our bodies will react to outside stimulus before it even happens. That message, if picked up soon enough, can be translated and may seem paranormal. It's more a case of super nature, rather than supernatural.

In tests into Bio Feedback in various labs, a computer was showing a series of images randomly images of kittens, puppies, and all things nice and the skin's resistance was seen to fall. The electrical charge of the skin lowered and with one random picture of a disturbing nature, the skin resistance climbed sharply.

So what, you may ask?

As the trial continued it was seen that the skin resistance was reacting before the random computer generated image appeared. For some reason still unknown the skin was pulling information from somewhere and sending the message to the brain and reacting accordingly before the events actually occurred. Of course this was only milliseconds in advance, but with some test subjects, they were reacting to something that had not happened yet. So we are left wondering how and why?

People walk into a house and get a chill, a sense they don't like it. Is this their bodies' way of telling them that there is something not quite right? Even though the other physical senses cannot see, hear, smell, or touch the disturbance doesn't mean it's still not there. Real estate agents will be aware that approx 70% of customers purchasing residential property will make that life-changing decision firstly on the way the property makes them feel.

Learning to listen to your gut instinct is vital and any police detective worth his salt will tell you he listens to that instinct from years of experience. We are continually trying to get good equipment and develop it. But if you don't have the gut instinct of where to place it, what good it is? It would be a shot in the dark. Sharpen that inner voice and you will begin to see results.

Technology Limitations: what each piece of equipment is capable of doing and under what circumstances.

Environmental Factors and interference with equipment

The environment will try and trick you all the time. Watch out for those power lines, the man-made EMF that can appear and disappear, and the GMFs. Remember that an EMF field will change once we enter a room. Be cautious and track down the causes of those fields and investigate from there. Some say that thunderstorms have a factor during the investigation, producing more activity. We have never encountered this -- and we've worked with industrial ion generators producing huge amounts of negative ions in a room and never found any correlation to activity.

Some have suggested that the humid climate will produce more ghosts. Not true either as there are many spirits to be found in the Middle East, just no volunteers outside of the armed forces to investigate the places we need to be though. But in the Middle East the Jinn are seen as being the main culprit of paranormal phenomenon.

The Islamic faith doesn't really identify with ghosts per se but rather believes in Jinn. Having experienced a case in which Jinn were involved, I can see why. I have never experienced anything as lacking principles as it did. Nothing of the western metaphysical or religious cultural remedy for spirits worked -- it was like water running off a duck's backside. The equipment was fried and we were treading on dangerous ground. I'm still working on developing a solution for these and I have been very reluctant to deal with a case containing these elements until more work has been done. But as the world becomes smaller and people migrate to other parts of the world to start a new way of life, sometimes these entities will travel with them and I know sooner or later I will have to deal with them again.

Battery drain and theory

The battery drain theory has been around for some time now. I'm not sure where it actually came from but it has been proposed that spirits take the energy from the batteries to help manifest. They consume the power and then can appear or another problem can be that the cold environment can severely disrupt a cheap battery's life cycle. We have had temperature issues before with batteries but have never experienced battery drain followed by an appearance of the thief in question. We have found it more of a hindrance. They can hit our equipment and cause us great annoyance and we cannot capture any proof.

One such incident occurred in 2000 back in Ireland at a location called Gillhall in County Down. We were setting up an experiment with cameras on a bridge where a horse and carriage had been reported to cross. Devilment was in the air -- something was taking a great interest in our work, but we staggered the cameras over three points of the bridge and set about our work. The first camera died in moments of beginning the experiment, the second moments after that, and the third got two more shots off before it too was dead.

The pictures were later developed and camera three caught the image of a figure approaching its position. The flash produced UV causing photons to become excited and burst from the atom that caused our figure to go into a stage of fluorescence. In that second we caught it before the camera battery died. The fluorescence effect is common with the introduction of UV to an area but they will back away with continual stimulus as the UV and in some cases the IR (depending on the type of entity) can cause issues for them.

But this is where we can understand such stories as the white lady that have made an appearance in nearly every castle across Europe at any onetime. They are not formed enough in that stage usually to determine their gender, but stories grow up around them and most times due to these stories the 'Lady' will become labeled. But this first test led to the birth of the full spectrum camera, which is a common term in the paranormal community.

An introduction to Magnetic waves

Mixed magnetic and electromagnetic fields pass through our brains throughout the course of any given day. The EMF frequency band is huge and we can only appreciate a small fraction. We live in an environment that is magnetically dense and has never been faced by any other human since our early development. Research conducted in 2005 suggests that both low-frequency natural geomagnetic fields (GMFs) and man-made electromagnetic fields (EMFs) can induce a number of biological, neuro-physiological and behavioral changes in humans.

Fluctuations in such fields can lead to the onset of abnormal behavior of vulnerable psychiatric subjects, which suggested a stimulation to produce epileptic activity in the brain, as well as other less significant occurrences. Recent tests into Bio Feedback have shown our skin reacts to outside stimulus before the conscious mind becomes aware of the threat. If we interfere with this ability, what ramifications will bleed from this?

Studies have shown that stimulation of the auditory cortex can induce hallucinations of speech and sounds in patients suffering from schizophrenia. Similar brain areas involved in processing visual and auditory stimuli from the outside world are also adapted to help produce instances of hallucination without any external stimulus.

A series of weak but very complex electromagnetic fields can be used with the potential to influence the human conscious experience. It's believed the field complexity rather than the large amounts of electromagnetic fields is an important factor for producing these types of experiences and is suggested to be rare in nature. Levels typically used within laboratory tests are generally in the range of10 nT-

1,000 nT (Nano Tesla). It should be noted the effects of this stimulus are not instantaneous and seem to result from constant exposure to these fields over a prolonged time period. More about these EMF fields and the complex effects they have on humans can be read in Albert Budden's book 'Electric UFO'.

It's been suggested in some fields that 10% of the modern population is electrically hypersensitive. This is something to bear in mind in any modern day case and should be searched for with the new and developing equipment listed below.

Compasses and EMF

Your compass is a cheap but effective subtle EMF device. Small disturbances in the EMF will make the needle react, but its limitations in a dark room are an obvious problem, never mind portability during the investigation, as each model will need time to settle. However, should you get lost, it's handy to get home where you should then pack it into a nearby cupboard and never go investigating again.

EMF Detectors

Most modern EMF detectors are not sensitive enough to pick up on the magnetic field coming off a 9V battery. As suggested before, they are designed to monitor man-made electrics which is mighty useful should you be woken in a panic with a heavy sweat by the spirit of an old TV set which was murdered by a brick or washing machine maybe ditched in some empty parking lot. But apart from that they really don't serve any purpose for serious research.

This research is about the subtleties that are at the lower ends not found in the man-made overhead power lines. Our attention recently was drawn to a device at nearly US$400 that recorded high levels of EMF and on a sub note stated it was useful to paranormal investigators. With that mindset a Bentley Continental Twin Turbo would be very useful as well and we'll take two, but realistically not only could we not afford the automobiles, we would have no need for it, much like an ashtray on a motorcycle. This reflects back onto knowing the capabilities of the equipment, but more importantly knowing what it is you are looking for.

TriField Meters

TriField made a wonderful little device called the Natural EMF. It was sensitive enough to detect those small changes and should someone come up with a recording device and data logger to correlate questions and responses they may be onto something. On several locations around the world we have seen the lower end EMF more suitably known as ELF (Extra Low Frequency) fluctuate suggesting a response to questions being asked by researchers.

However hand-held radios and various other signal generators can affect them since they made a recent modification to the sensor making it even more sensitive.

As long as you can account for other signals, they still remain a personal favorite. Its sister model, the TriField EMF, will register man-made signals from various areas and can show those troublesome signals and help track down their origins.

Geomagnetic Field Detectors

Geomagnetic phenomenon should also be monitored, but to save yourself some cash you can purchase the TriField Natural EMF meter that has a setting to measure such a disturbance. But the rise and fall of geomagnetic phenomena comes in slow waves shifting over time. Unless you are on top of an active fault line and the house is falling down around you and the ground shakes up and down or may be side to side, you would not need the meter to tell you your experiencing an earthquake. However if you did, I would suggest finding the remains of the cupboard you put the compass into and place your meter in the same place and take the hint. Paranormal hunting may not be for you.

Temperature Guns – Ambient and Surface

In the early days the temperature guns were seen as the latest craze, but people didn't realize they were useless for finding cold spots as the signal passed straight through the cold spot and sent you back the temperature of the wall, door, or window. The cold spots eluded the investigator, but more recently came the introduction of the ambient monitor that gave you both surface and ambient air temperature at the same time on one meter. Finally someone somewhere was getting it, but the next stage for these are to evolve or even change out entirely and we should look at wireless temperature monitors filtering back to a data logger which could record all night, even over the course of a week, and see the patterns before a team goes into investigate.

Does a tree make a noise when it falls in the wood and no one is there to hear it? Likewise is a house haunted if no one is there to experience it? The answer is, of course, yes.

A Real-Life Story from Barry

A test conducted back in County Armagh in Ireland had us monitor a house that presented the occupants with no other alternative but to leave. Ten years had passed since anyone lived there and when we arrived, the TV, furniture, and kitchenware were still in the home, the house was simply abandoned and left with its contents.

As we stayed outside, we mapped the building on the hood of the car and the phone rang inside. We ignored it and it rang several times again. From outside, it was apparent that the wires had been cut and on further investigation there wasn't even a phone in the house. But as we laid out sound recording devices in the property and retreated to the road a good half a mile away the devices picked up the furniture being dragged around the floors. The entity from this location that was being investigated became troublesome when it followed a friend and fellow investigator to their newly built home and started to present the same activity there as he did and in the original location under investigation and we had to deal with him and send him packing.

Thermal Cameras (For Alt Explanations)

A faulty heating system can cause no end of trouble and for those that frighten easily can led to many sleepless nights. But should pipes be making noises under the floorboards and walls a good thermal camera will easily put this to rest in the minds of the occupant. Their focal ranges can be limiting but for work no further than ten feet, but enough detail will be seen to allow the user the ability to come to a good conclusion either way.

Infrared Video Cameras

The current market has approximately ten reasonable IR video recorders both in quality and price range. Most are designed to enhance your ability to record in a reduced light situation or no light level. Most of these technologies developed from warfare, like most of the technology we see today -- the double-edged sword. Recent research form the UK has indicated that even such light stimulus from IR has an effect on the manifestation scale. Our work is starting to indicate those there maybe two camps, one that is effected by the infrared and one effected by the ultraviolet. But night vision in the battlefield is by far still much more improved than that available on your household video recorder. There would be more terrorists in the world today if the armed forces where relying on IR illumination from modern video camera manufactures.

One account from the metaphysical circuit within the UK has stated that IR from our cameras acts like acid on our skin during particular stages of manifestation. This of course once again leaves us up a creek without a paddle. How can we film in darkness without our night vision?

It seems there may be an answer in low lux cameras. These cameras are designed to capture low light and enhance the light available so we can observe the visible light spectrum without placing extreme light conditions into the investigation. The full spectrum section of this chapter will explain the situation with the introduction and detrimental effects of introducing UV into an investigation.

The advancement of cameras -- due in part from 'Greater Vision Technologies' who have been developing new low lux cameras with the capabilities of 120 frames per second and a 12 million pixel camera which can be linked to any standard DVR system or straight into a USB in any laptop -- simply means we are capable of recording into the higher ranges of the UV of approximately 260nm.

Where possible, we would recommend a camera that can see as much in low light as possible without producing its own light source. Applying a red light to the environment you are filming can help greatly with materialization and filming in the dark environment, this in itself was a great way of bridging the divide and again we borrow this from the old style mediums.

IR Illuminators

The illuminators will help boost the range of the IR capabilities of your limited cameras. A good manufacturer should be able to supply you a compact unit with a broad beam range down to approx 800nm. Watch out for those that also come with a dimmer switch -- these can be very useful in a corridor where you tend to get an excess of reflected IR back into your lens. In open areas you can light them right up and can boost the range of your handheld unit sometimes up to 150%.

Full Spectrum Technology

"Turn your face to the sun and the shadows fall behind you."
-Maori Proverb

Light is a form of electromagnetic energy that moves in measurable waves. Our eyes have evolved and are only capable of seeing a small segment of the light spectrum known as the visible light; shorter and longer wavelengths are not visible. Cosmic, gamma, X-rays, and UV light are found in the shorter light spectrum, while infrared and radio waves are in the longer light spectrum. We theorize that some humans have the ability to see a little further into either end of the spectrum than most. UV energy radiates between 180 nanometer (nm) to 400nm wavelengths in the narrow region between X-rays and just below the violet end of the visible-light spectrum.

The region known as near ultraviolet, or UV-A, extends from 320-400nm -- most black lights operate in this region but a small portion of the population are overly sensitive to radiation in this region of the spectrum and may experience adverse effects. For example, some people experience "blue haze" which is caused by looking at sources of long wave UV due to the fluorescent effects in the ocular media. This is why it is extremely important when using and experimenting with this light source that you wear proper eye protection.

Eye protection is recommended and absolutely essential for anyone working with short-wave ultraviolet light. Some safety glasses protect eyes from harmful UV radiation emitted from UV lamps by absorbing 99.9% of the UV radiation up to 385 nm. Another added benefit is the elimination of the "blue haze" effect from long wave UV.

We have witnessed in the field that some entities in later stages of materialization will be illuminated by certain wavelengths of UV, reflecting back the same wavelengths that they are illuminated with and transforming some of these wavelengths into longer ones. When an entity is caught like this it is said to FLUORESCE. This is what can happen in the paranormal research fields, as the spirit begins manifestation, it reflects back the long wave and can be caught in those milliseconds as the shutter closes.

Understanding this process may lead us to understand why animals are better at seeing entities than we are. Although we can sense them, the animals can really see them, as we believe some become visible in the UV spectrum rather than the commonly held belief that we can see them in the infrared spectrum.

We do wonder why our kids can see spirits in our homes and such. Recent research confirmed that as we grow older the UV filter protecting our eyes thickens as we age. Therefore the UV we would have seen into, as a child would no longer be visible to us. Is it possible this may be the reason as our children grow older they lose touch with their invisible friends and bogeymen that slip out from the closets?

UV fluorescence is a common trait in nature, however it is one we cannot see due to our limited vision. Nature has more beauties to offer us if we could only see. Animals and insects can see further into the IR and UV spectrum and can aid them in their daily lives such as hunting, mating, and general survival. So why has the top of the food chain become so limited?

Vision occurs when light enters the eye and is absorbed by specialized cells located in the back of the eye. These cells respond to the light and send a signal to the brain that is translated into sight. The color perceived by the brain is determined by the wavelength of light reflected. In other words, objects do not actually have color they simply reflect light of a particular wavelength that our brain perceives as color.

In all mammals, the retina, located at the back of the eye, consists of two types of light sensitive cells called rods and cones. Rods function in the absence, or near absence, of light and permit vision in darkness. Cones function in full light and permit daytime and color vision. The paper-thin retina contains about 130 light receptors and around 6 million of these cones allow us to distinguish some 8 million colors. The remaining rods only detect black and white. They allow night vision and after an hour of darkness, become 75,000 times more sensitive.

However the human eye is protected by a filter that contains a series of low molecular compounds that block about 99 percent of UV light from entering the eye. This filter protects our eye and allows us to focus more sharply on finer detail. The trade-off for having this filter is a severe loss of sensitivity to short wavelength colors, especially those in the UV spectrum.

Scientists discovered this secret color world of UV in the 1950s as they studied the world of plants that offered a two tone color range quite unlike the type we see with our own eyes. It has been commonly known that bees can see into the UV spectrum and this two-tone effect has helped both the bee and plant during pollination.

In the age of 35mm it was known that particular cameras had the ability to shoot into the UV spectrum due to the lack of filters on the flashgun. The film was also vital in this matter, as it had to respond to light from the UV-A region of the light spectrum. Its only nemesis was the glass in the lens that was a natural blocker to the UV above 350nm approx.

We discovered by sheer accident that the images we were capturing in a haunted location in Ireland that coincided with severe battery drain might well have been real paranormal phenomenon. The UV produced by the flash caused this fluorescence to occur and in a second the 35mm film captured it.

But before we all run out and start buying up equipment we must understand there is a manifestation scale which I have been observing for almost ten years, which, once understood, will help you also in capturing true paranormal phenomenon.

A word of warning though: if we consider that a majority of hauntings occurs at night (as children famously claim when they're scared), the fact of the matter is that they came from the darkness. The natural lack of UV in this environment is a key factor for some of these types of disturbances. I have noticed that the introduction of UV into a haunted environment will greatly reduce paranormal phenomenon as these entities move away with great haste from the light source.

If activity is occurring in the physical realm then you can quite effectively assume that they will respond to the fluorescence theory and will be caught on the device altered to accept UV-A, but you are going to be limited in how many shots you have. Once the flashgun is activated they will move away.

They key is to wait for activity in the physical realm and only then. Using flash photography both digital and in 35mm before such an event will only ruin your attempts to truly photograph paranormal phenomenon. So place the camera on a tripod and get to know your equipment run tests and see how well the devices perform in low light and if you can make the necessary adjustments to gain the most from your equipment.

I'm aware of folks that take shots without the tripods and this I feel is a grave mistake, as you cannot properly analyze the photos. Unless taken on a tripod, each photo will not give you the same perspective no matter how steady a hand you have. All it takes is a half-inch movement and you no longer have a copy of the original. But when practicing with UV photography or IR photography at night you should be using a tripod anyhow. Using the flash will only interfere with your findings as explained.

Ion Counters and Weather Stations

The issue of the ion monitoring came into play during an investigation back in Ireland. On a specific location the strange feeling of fatigue and weakness came over people, which led to a great mystery and obvious legends developed about both inside and outside the property.

On one of those detective hunches I wanted to monitor the weather, suspecting there may indeed be an outside force at play. It seemed a long shot, however, as the strange feelings were only experienced during the investigations, suggesting that weather was not responsible and that the entity we were tracking was being very sagacious.

So on the next available visit to the site, which was a few hundred feet above sea level, a weather station monitored the environmental patterns. The weather was fine and clear and with all the instruments in place the investigation began.

Around two hours into the investigation an ultraviolet light source was introduced and within three minutes the weather station alarmed the team to a distinct change. The device was warning of a storm and indicated severe weather, yet outside the building the weather remained still and clear; in fact, for the next several days, the weather remained the same.

Within twenty minutes, fatigue struck and the feeling of weakness was very apparent, along with a similar feeling in the pit of my stomach which has since became my internal alarm to let me know if such activity is occurring without having to reach for equipment.

The weather station continued to tell of a storm until we were around two miles from the location and once again it read clear weather. But each time the experiment was applied and the environmental patterns changed it took a long time for the body to recover from the effects.

With this clue in hand more research led to a theory that certain locations can house Inhumans, particular types of which are capable of manipulating the localized environmental pattern and have adverse effects on those investigating. I have seen this pattern on numerous locations around the world and have been able to track the activity as it happens.

A stark rise in positive ions is the first clue. The quicker your team is able to detect this the more time you have to move out of the location. But for most teams you will have to settle for the less expensive weather station, as the rise in positive ions will be indicated on the weather station as an approaching storm. This disturbance will be in the immediate area, and this will have as described an effect on the atmospheric pressure. As the pressure continues to lower this can have an effect on the individual (some people are more prone to the effects than others as the blood pressure will drop). This may also have an effect on our first line of defense -- our own immune system and therefore we become open its effects.

But as seen in a location in the European Union, this drop will continue and place the person into total circulatory collapse -- effectively you can die of a heart attack. A silent assassin you might say and one, which has for a long time gone, unnoticed in France. Its mark is untraceable to those that don't know what they are looking for. But here you have a little piece of the story to help you develop your own research with some guidelines that have already been observed and measured, which is a rare event indeed within this field. However due to the nature of the phenomenon it is too large to try and reverse and at this time all we can do should we come across this activity is to mark it and set the clock running to move away from the core of the activity and to a safe zone.

But the ion count does not end there. I was recently in conversation with my friend and engineer about what the new phenomenon the low lux high end UV DVR cameras were capturing. Balls of light were appearing in higher ranges of the UV and well beyond the capabilities of the human observer. These glowing lights would appear and slowly close in on themselves, ghostly lights about the size of a tennis ball. The cameras depict these lights in different colors in direct relation to the range within the UV spectrum they appear in -- some red, some yellow and green.

How and why these are appearing remains unclear. These lights have been reported in the séance rooms of old and because we could not see them we wrote them off as imaginary, yet here we are suddenly witnessing these balls of energy suddenly form and slowly collapse usually within seconds. Brazilian medium 'O Medium Mirabelli' also reported similar activity. She performed in front of respected witnesses who observed these claims including the President of Brazil, the Secretary of State, two professors of medicine, 72 doctors, 12 engineers, 36 lawyers, 89 public officials, 25 military personnel, 52 bankers, 128 merchants, 22 dentists, along with members of religious orders -- all of whom reported the paranormal phenomenon.

We speculated the balls of energy where indeed a form of energy and are known within quantum physics as a fold back, which simply refers to a collapse of an energy field. The footage is remarkable to witness, though I would imagine to most they look like unremarkable, colored balls of light, but in serious paranormal circles they are a wonderful breakthrough that begs for more research.

Another story was related to me about light breezes being felt in rooms sealed from drafts. During paranormal experiments these light breezes could be felt on one's bare skin. It was speculated that these may be a direct result of the collapse of the energy fields and the breeze is actually the rush of negative ions that will rush to matter once the field totally collapses. You can feel the same type of breeze form by holding your hand in front of an ion generator. In one case these light breezes were felt and the ion counter was brought into the investigation and sure enough the ions were on a sharp rise and fall as theorized.

Unfortunately the camera was unable to be utilized as it was otherwise occupied filming another part of the case location. But once again small clues and hunches can lead to great advancements. We feel excited to be on the edge of something which we hope will change the way we research in the future and understand paranormal phenomenon.

Digital Recorders - Analog Recorders and 360-Degree Microphones

There are a great number of digital voice recorders on the market and quality will depend on how much you have got to spend. Quality is an issue and should not be underestimated. The new age of digital voice recorder has studio quality .wav formats and some on the market have wonderful microphone systems, such as the Zoom H2 with four on-board microphones offering a 360-degree angle recording facility covering the entire room. The files are stored on an SD card and are easily transferred to the computer. Once applied to quality software you can see the greater signal strength depicted on the graph display and know where the sounds are coming from within the room.

With the advancements in technology we have no reason to fall back to analog. The machine noise from these old devices led to the misreading of Electrical Voice Phenomena (EVP) and caused audio matrixing. Some older researchers may disagree with that and say that it's the noise that helped the EVP to materialize, but we have other devices today to take care of that called noise generators.

Friedrich Jürgenson, a pioneer of EVP work in the mid 20th century, was a Swedish bird watcher who recorded a series of voices on a tape deck he had purposely bought to record bird calls. On playback he heard voices that could not be explained and with more work he recorded many more over the following four years of his work within EVP circles. Many of the voices were using foreign languages. Most of the voices were barely intelligible and almost completely drowned by tape hiss, which was a continual problem with the open reel recorders of the time. The later additions to the tape decks helped but the machine noise continued to remains a problem until we got to the digital age.

White Noise and various other colors – including natural noise

Konstantin Raudive, a Latvian psychologist who was living in Germany, published the most interesting evidence ever gathered on white noise generators in 1968. Raudive discovered that recordings could be made by speaking directly into the microphone and by recording from a radio tuned to random "White Noise" interference, or by connecting the recorder to a crystal diode set with a very short aerial. Each time, soft extraneous voices were heard. Six years after the first initial test, Raudive recorded more than 70,000 conversations of this kind.

Noise generators are coming back into the fold for investigation. A recent piece of software available on the Internet for free is called the EVP assistant and was designed by the EVP Research Association UK. These devices supply frequencies in the audible range during your investigation and can supply all manner of interesting findings. We have used the EVP assistant on many investigations and within fifteen minutes voices are heard emanating from the edges of the room, just outside the range of the IR cameras. In one sitting up to 20 people confirmed hearing the voices.

The program allows the user to select from different background noises such as white noise, pink noise, brown noise, waterfall, and up to the very effective Spiricom. The Spiricom noise was taken from original recordings by George Meek and William O'Neil but due to the frequency of this noise, we do not recommend listening to it for long periods of time.

Should you decide to use this we do recommend reading the instructions in full and understanding the warnings that are indicated by the inventors. This is still a shady part of research and much still has to be learned from this program and other machines like it.

Chapter 5

Alternative Explanations

Common Occurrence and Coincidence

*"Twenty years from now you will be more disappointed
by the things you didn't do than by the ones you did do.
So throw off the bowlines. Sail away from the safe
harbor. Catch the trade winds in your sails.
Explore. Dream. Discover"*

MARK TWAIN

Throughout your investigations you will no doubt encounter some things that truly cannot be explained. However this does not mean that you should not at least try to come up with a possible alternative explanation for these otherwise paranormal occurrences.

When hearing claims of the paranormal that you are going to investigate, it is paramount that you get inside the mind of the person reporting these claims.

Do they want to believe in the activity being that of a ghost so much that they are willing to suspend the reality of the situation? This insistent belief could arise from the grief experienced by the loss of a loved one, by a commitment to preconceived notion, belief in old stories and traditions, or perhaps some are even driven by the hopes of financial gain should their place be deemed "haunted."

In many cases people have been told a story for so long about ghostly activity in an area that it does in fact take on a life of its own, with or without and significant evidence of the paranormal. This is especially true in terms of places that have any sort of cultural or historical significance as people sometimes cling to these stories with a guarded close mindedness and blind faith.

Very important aspects to any investigation are field experiments and recreation attempts.

In many cases reported sounds like footsteps and banging can be attributed to a heating or ventilation system or water pipes. Its to your benefit to always check out the basement of a location even if there are no reports there as it many cases you can more easily pinpoint the sources of these stray sounds before they echo throughout a home or building.

Another common culprit for the sound of footsteps is the layout of wooden floorboards. Are there floorboards that are connected in such a way that a step in one direction yields a pop or squeak in another direction? A simple and thorough walk throughout the room of this reported phenomena is all it takes to undermine this claim.

Flickering lights can usually be the result of bad wiring and should only be looked into by a licensed electrician. As an investigator, you can at least check the switches without removing the cover plate, to see if they are loose when you toggle them on or off. Could there be a faulty switch or problem within the wiring harness?

Cold spots or hot spots can be investigated with the use of an ambient temperature thermometer, a surface temperature gun or a thermal camera. (See more on items in the Equipment section.)

An of course when investigating claims it is always possible that you may be dealing with forces unseen, and I don't mean ghosts. In this case I am talking about Infrasound.

Infrasound is an inaudible, low frequency sound wave that runs from zero to twenty hertz and can be generated by many things both natural and man-made.

Some objects capable of producing infrasound include Church organs, electrical equipment, jets, and ventilation systems to name a few.

In nature infrasound occurs from severe weather, and natural disasters such as earthquakes, tornados and volcanic activity. Changes in the ionosphere in response to storms also coincide with the ion charge noted in some hauntings.

Many animals such as crocodiles, tigers, hippos and whales to name a few, use infrasound for communication, as it is a great tool for covering long distances and for defending territory which can span great distances. Elephants in particular use their feet to produce infrasound capable of traveling hundreds of miles through solid ground to the herd.

Animals are known to perceive natural disasters and flee before they happen, this may be in part to their interpretation of infrasound waves.

These sound waves can sometimes make objects in a room vibrate and when they hit the eardrum, the brain may interpret these waves, but only a certain and very small range of them, as sound. Mostly they manifest as a sense of movement, often rendering the person feeling strangely alert, uneasy or with a queasy stomach.

Most often the brain interprets infrasound in such a way that stimulates the fight or flight response; causing the heart to race, the hair on the back of your neck and arms to rise, and for the sensation of chills, along with the heightened awareness of a temperature change.

Infrasound also has a tendency to gather up where the troughs and peaks of sound waves overlap, and dissipate where troughs and peaks cancel each other out. Thus causing isolated spots of infrasound. This may coincide with the "cold spot" phenomena that is so widely reported in the paranormal field.

If something, be it a piece of equipment or natural phenomena is responsible for generating the infrasound, it would tend to coincide with stories of reported activity within the same area of a location as infrasound is known to pool.

Large and empty areas made of stone, such as castles and basements, often lack furniture, home decor and other such objects which normally help to absorb these imperceptible sound waves, thus there is a heightened potential for these sensations which are so frequently associated with a haunting to occur.

Older buildings often have a thicker wall construction, which aides in the resonation of infrasound and sound in general. Hence why we can hear echoes so much better in these conditions. Also why places designed for great acoustics, such as opera houses and theaters, may also lend to this not so paranormal event.

Surprisingly infrasound also plays a role in the shadows that are often reported being seen out of the corner of one's eye.

The human eyeball itself resonates at the frequency of eighteen or nineteen hertz depending whom you talk to and what study they conducted. One such study documented, by the good folks at NASA; putting monkeys into space and endorsing Tang since your mother was a child, or more specifically the 1960's, depending if you are my age or not, found the eyeball to resonate at 18 hertz.

NASA had to do this to ensure the safety of the astronauts upon the immense sound waves created by the force needed so that Americans could play golf on the moon. (I am not sure if they did these frequency tests before the monkeys went into space; it probably depended on where the animal rights activists were at the time.)

The quivering effect on the eyeball is just enough to cause the brain to register movement and blurs within the peripheral range of vision, which is otherwise known as vision smearing or smudging.

The fact that the eyeball resonates within the range of infrasound is particularly intriguing as it also may explain why the quick blurs and shadows that are often reported in many ghost sightings are reported to have been seen out of the corner of the eye.

It's interesting to point out that infrasound is not always experienced by everyone present. It has been reported that out of 100 people, only two or three may be affected be infrasonic waves.

So how do you know if infrasound is what is causing the reported paranormal activity?

Purchasing specialized equipment for the testing of infrasound is one way to cross reference data gained during investigations as well as a great tool to legitimize experiences and rule out the stealthily intrusive infrasound.

Infrasound can be analyzed and measured with certain sound meters and vibration sensors.

As an investigator it is imperative that we continue to probe for alternative explanations to what some claim to be paranormal. You may find that keeping a list of new discoveries and plausible theories may be helpful as you gather new information during your research and investigations.

Chapter 6

A Place To Hunt

Finding and Accessing Haunted Locations

*"Don't be afraid that your life will end,
be afraid that it will never begin!"*

ANONYMOUS

So you have your gear, you have a team … now what?

Finding a haunted location to investigate isn't as easy as you might think. Short of living in a haunted location yourself, you have to do some groundwork to find a place.

Graveyards have long been a popular location for people in the field. However, we suggest you skip the graveyards and leave them be. It is important to realize that just because there are human remains at a location, there isn't necessarily a reason to believe that their spirits remain there as well. Not to mention it is illegal in most places to be in cemeteries after hours. It is also outdoors, so contamination is a problem for many aspects of a thorough investigation. In short, let those in the graveyards rest in peace.

Local hot spots, area hotels, theaters, and residences with paranormal claims are very appealing places to try and gain access. It is sometimes difficult to get permission to investigate at these places, however.

The best way to go about it is finding out who manages or owns the location and proceed from there with a professional letter of intent stating who you are, how long you have been established, what it is that you are precisely trying to do, and the means by which you are going to go about it. Always be respectful and courteous, as this will go a long way in not only getting permission, but also establishing yourself as a professional and not just some crazy person with a video camera and a tape recorder.

A great place to start is within your own team or circle of friends. Do any of them have a place of their own or perhaps know of a relative or acquaintance that believes their place to be haunted and would give you the opportunity to look into it?

Social networking on websites like MySpace, Facebook, and various paranormal sites also offer the chance not only to talk to others in the field, but also make yourself and your team accessible to those who may be looking for a local team to offer their services. You can also put out bulletins and place postings, all of which can start a word-of-mouth advertising campaign for you and your team.

Placing ads in local papers and on community bulletin boards around town is also effective way to let the public know of your services. We suggest placing an ad in a smaller, artsy newspaper rather than in the mainstream one. You are much more likely to attract the attention of an open-minded individual who may be in need of your help.

Stay consistent in your investigative techniques, stay true to the field, and treat others with respect and you and your team could go very far in the paranormal field.

Chapter 7

Understanding Your Clients

Interviewing Questions, Techniques, and Red Flags

"There are hundreds of languages in the world,
but a smile speaks them all."

ANONYMOUS

Once a potential client invites you to investigate a location for them it is important that you make the proper approach and ask the right questions in order to prepare yourself and your team for the case.

Once a potential client invites you to investigate a location for them, it is important that you make the proper approach and ask the right questions in order to prepare yourself and your team for the case.

Simple things must be considered, such as logistics. Is the location suitable for an investigation and deserving of one? To determine the worth of the case, ask the following questions:

- How frequently have the events in question been occurring?
- Have they been occurring within a recent time period?
- Have the people reporting the events made any attempt to disprove the claims, or at least considered any alternative explanations to the activity?
- Have they recorded any activity themselves?
- Do they posses a journal or a rough timeline of the activity that could help you in your investigation?
- What is it the client is asking you to do for them?

After you ask these initial questions, you will have a better idea if a true investigation is indeed warranted. Of course, if you are just starting out, even a small case with lesser occurrences and frequency can still be an exciting one and worth your time, as you need to hone your skills in the field. Even one repetitious claim with incredible frequency can be worth the trip.

It is also important to consider where the case is located, how long it will take you, and how much it will cost you to get there. Since you are providing a volunteer service in the name of scientific research, you should not be charging the client and thus must absorb the costs of your own equipment, travel, and time.

Once the case is deemed worthy of an investigation, you should contact the client and further gain their trust. Assure them that their identity will be kept confidential should they wish it to be. Give them background information on yourself and your team members, and outline what it is you are hoping to do in this field. If you are planning someday to publish your research, for instance, be sure that you have their expressed, written consent.

Put the client at ease and reassure them that you and your team will be respectful of their dwelling and that no harm will come to any of it. Someone allowing you into his or her home, or any other place they represent, is not something that should be taken lightly.

At this point it is a good time to ask further questions about the case in regards to the dwelling itself and its occupants.

The following questions should be asked so that you have a better understanding of who is present, what is happening, and what alternatives may exist to help explain the occurrences in question.

- What are the names and ages of people living in the house?

- What medications are the people in the house taking?

(Specifically this pertains to the people who have
been present at or who have had the experiences. Common side effects of said medications can be found easily
through on-line resources.)

- Is there any illegal drug or alcohol use? If so, were
  these being used at the times of the claims?

  (You will be surprised at some of the answers you
  will receive.)

- Does anyone within the dwelling at the time of
  the reported activities have a psychiatric history
  that needs to be considered?
- Do the people reporting the claims have any religious affiliations? And to what extent do they take
  their beliefs?
- Are there pets in the house?

  (This is important to know as pets can contribute
  to many aspects of items being moved or knocked
  over within the home without the homeowner being aware of it, among other things. Also check to
  see if the pets themselves were present during the
  supposed paranormal activity and if they had any
  reaction to it.)

- What movies, television programs, or books have they recently been exposed to?

  (Some claims will coincide remarkably with something they have been recently exposed to and therefore were subconsciously more aware of. Other claims will simply be the result of an over active imagination.)

- Have any of the people in the dwelling recently lost a loved one?
- Have they ever invited a psychic or medium into the area?
- Have they ever held a séance at the location in question or used a Ouija board or similar device in the area?
- Does anyone have a theory as to what may be going?

Compare the stories and reported claims of all people in the home separately and look for discrepancies as well as similarities. Once you complete the interview you should agree upon and set a date and time for the investigation, and be sure you and your team members are there promptly on that date. Also set up a scout date so that you may arrive at a pre-arranged time and walk through the location thoroughly with the client one more time before bringing in the team.

Be sure to draft some simple paperwork in which it is stated that you and your team (list all members by name) are being granted permission at the specific address of the location, on a certain date and time by the client, who is a representative or owner of the property and is granting you permission to conduct the investigation as it was discussed between you. The client, yourself, and a witness should all sign this document. Be sure to keep it on file and not disregard it immediately after the case. Keep detailed records of all your investigations!

Now that you have conducted your interviews, gained the clients' trust, and obtained expressed, written consent to hold the investigation, you should go over the answers you were given and look for clues.

- Are there patterns to the disturbances?
- Is there someone who is present during each occurrence?
- Are the claims all coming from one person?
- What is it your client is looking for?

  (Perhaps they are seeking validation, answers, comfort or help.)

- Could there also be an ulterior motive for inviting you and your group in?

With the rise of paranormal television programs and events, there is a serious publicity factor to be considered. Be aware of outside motivations for a place to be christened "haunted."

Before investigation night you should also do some preliminary research regarding the history of the building, the land, and the people who have resided and do reside there. You may be able to obtain some of this information from the client, the Internet, or your local library and newspaper archives.

All of these questions should be asked and their answers seriously considered so that you are as aware of every possible situation as you can be. Being well prepared is not one of the flashier parts of the investigation, but it is one of the most important.

Chapter 8

First Impressions

Scouting a Possibly Haunted Location

"Many of our fears are tissue-paper-thin, and a single courageous step would carry us clear through them."

BRENDAN FRANCIS

We believe it is very important to come back to an investigation location after the initial client interview to scout the area in a more relaxed setting. This will allow you to form a more complete impression of the case and the reported activity.

Other steps to take:

If you have a team member with some legitimate sensitivity, perhaps you could bring them so that they may evaluate the place as well.

- Have the client give you a walkthrough of the entire location, focusing on the areas where the reported activity had occurred. Make sure the location is safe for yourself and the team.
- Look for any hazards that may impede your investigation. Loose floorboards and steps can be a real problem in the dark. Just be aware of their location and make sure you relay the information to your team.
- Be cognizant of the location's size as it compares to the number of investigators that will be present during the case. You do not want to overload a smaller location as it will frustrate your investigators and add to possible evidence contamination.
- Consider a centralized location for your base of operations, which should be a room with no reported activity where you can keep your equipment and set up your DVR system (More on this to follow in the Investigation Night Chapter).

- During your scouting period, be on the lookout for anything that could be fraudulent. Examine closely doors that reportedly open and close by themselves, look for hidden speakers or wires where noises or voices are reportedly heard. Do not forget that some people could be looking to cash in for publicity.
- Look over your notes again, look over your interviews, and look over the claims. See if you can come up with an initial theory of what you may be dealing with and why it may be there.
- Finally, reconfirm the date and time of your investigation and ensure that you have the necessary paperwork to cover yourself for legal issues should any arise.

Chapter 9

Lights Out – It's Investigation Night

What To Do and What Not To Do: That is the Question

"There are only two ways to live your life.
One is as though nothing is a miracle.
The other is as though everything is a miracle."

ALBERT EINSTEIN

Once you are about to begin your investigation be sure that you have effectively informed all of your team members about the reported activity and the location of said activity.

Typing out a one-paged report of accounts and locations can be helpful as you can give a copy to each team member to hold on to for the night, even if they just fold it up and stash it in their pocket for reference.

Be weary of onlookers and unwanted tag along investigators. Your team should be established and friends of friends should not be tagging along on the case. Nor should the client be inviting people over to watch as this will hinder your investigation as well as contribute to extra noise contamination.

If there is a predominant shared theory of what may be occurring it should be discussed and kept in mind throughout the night. Beware of tunnel vision- never forget to reassess your opinion and theory as the night progresses and evidence begins to mount. Experiences that you may have could direct you to another theory all together, so do not limit yourself.

Locate the area on the premises that you have determined would make a good base of operations. It should be close enough to activity so that you can easily access your equipment, yet not too close as to cause contamination every time someone needs something. Discuss a team plan, divvy up equipment and proceed with your investigative plan.

Be sure to use the right tools for the job, which may vary depending on the case, and even depending on the claims within the case. (See more on this in the Equipment Chapter) Depending on what it is you believe you are investigating, you should be trying the proper techniques to give yourself the best chance at capturing paranormal activity.

EVP sessions, digital photography, full spectrum photography, EMF detection as well as DVR recording and various other investigative techniques should be thoroughly conducted throughout the investigation in the appropriate areas of concern. Trigger objects, if applicable and approved by the client, should also be implemented, often set up in front of a DVR camera or mini DV recorder to monitor and record any movement. Be sure to get baseline readings where applicable with EMF detectors, Trifield meters, thermometers and the like as you will need a control test for comparative reasons should anomalous readings occur. As always, be on the look out for false positives.

Make sure you check back on the sheet so that you do not miss an opportunity to investigate every claim that was given to you. Make sure you didn't inadvertently misrepresent the claim or distort any of the factors of the claim.

Throughout the investigation try to remember that despite sensational reports of activity, you should remain skeptical.

Do not be too suggestive in interpreting your surroundings and ambient noises. If you really need to stretch to make an assumption that something is evidence of the paranormal, it really isn't.

Don't forget to look for clues as to Religious beliefs that may have not been voiced, evidence of occult activity, and always be examining the possibility of alternative explanations.

Many teams find it important to work is a set of two and not be in an area alone. This is good advice in larger areas where you may not be able to get to each other in case of an emergency. And by emergency we do not mean just something paranormal, but simply ordinary everyday emergencies that occur when one is tumbling around a strange location in the dark. In the case of dealing with a possibly ill-willed Inhuman however, you probably should have someone there with you.

It is also helpful to have an area set aside for investigators to meet up and decompress or exchange information. Usually this can be done at your base of operations, as it should be an area where there are no reports of activity. However you may want to have another area that is more remote so that you will not contaminate any evidence that other team members are trying to gather. It is also helpful to have an area sanctioned off as a sort of safety zone so that if things get too much for a team member they have a place they know they can retreat to.

If things do get to the point where the team has safety concerns due to activity it is important that you maintain your professionalism as best you can, as you do not want to alarm the client nor lose your credibility as a professional in the field.

If there is legitimate concern for the client's well being, they should be informed in a calm and collected manor. Retreating to a safe area or going outside will usually settle everyone down, help calm nerves and ease the situation.

As the night wears on and your time is running low, make sure you have done everything you have set out to do without losing sight of the big picture.

What do all the little happenings and paranormal occurrences add up to?

What are you dealing with? Is there one spiritual entity or more than one?

What is its nature? What does it want? Is there anything really going on at all?

After the case is over, do your best to make some detailed notes as soon as you can so that experiences and discoveries are not forgotten or the location of which becomes confused. Each piece of evidence garnered could prove to be very important.

Wrapping up your investigation should occur within the time allotted by your client. Be sure to gather all team members together and pack up each piece of your equipment. A checklist is helpful to make sure you leave nothing behind. Also have a case with a place for everything is helpful and ensures your equipment is taken care of during transport. Thank your client and go get some rest- you'll need it for evidence review.

Chapter 10

A Solid Foundation

Evidence Review - Building The Case

*"Life is not measured by the number of breaths we take,
but by the moments that take our breath away."*

ANONYMOUS

Once you have rested up from investigation night it will be time to review all that you and your team have gathered. This includes all the audio recorders, all the photographs, the videotapes and DVR footage. Depending on the length of your investigation, the thoroughness of your team, and the amount of equipment used, evidence review can add up to be a monumental task.

The best way to approach it is systematically. Dividing up the tasks amongst team members is also very helpful if possible. Certain team members may excel in an area where another may be weak; knowing the strengths and weaknesses of your teams' ability to review evidence will aid in dividing it amongst them.

For all types of evidence – the location at which it was gathered, investigators whom were present, time code and tape number if applicable – should be noted.

Personal experiences that occurred during the case as well as EMF fluctuations, Ion count increases, and temperature changes should also be noted for place and time if possible. This will prove useful in building a more complete case. Personal experiences such as being touched, seeing an object move or a spirit manifest, are considered very weak if evidence, if evidence at all, without something concrete to back it up. However, a personal experience that has been paired up to time and place along with an EVP, a disturbance in the EMF fields, and an anomalous photograph makes for an incredible paranormal package.

For those of you brand new to the field, let's take an elementary look at various types of equipment and what exactly you should be looking for.

Audio Recorders

If digital, they can be easily uploaded into audio software programs or simply played back on the recording device itself. Listening through a pair of quality headphones will increase your chances of hearing the faintest of whispers, but so will having a good audio recorder. Be sure to note where the EVP session was being conducted and who was present, all audio recorders should be slated, meaning the investigators should say where they are conducting the session and with whom they are investigating. Time of the session can also be useful as to pinpoint when events were happening and to cross-reference if anything else was occurring at the time.

As with every piece of evidence, be sure to note the time code it can be found at, and also include what you believe to hear within the EVP. Team members may have varying opinions and it is sometimes helpful not to mention your ideas to your teammates until they hear it for themselves and form their own idea. This way you don't predetermine their response.

Whispering is not encouraged during EVP sessions as it can create for confusion during evidence review. Talking in a lower voice or hushed tone is optimal. Be sure to direct your questions to whomever you think may be there and use an appropriate line of questioning to increase your chances of getting answers. Also be sure to open up the investigation to whoever or whatever else may be lurking in the darkness. A simple set of generic questions can be done should the possible identity of the spirit be unknown.

You should be listening intently for any voices or whispers that do not sound like that of the investigators present, or that do not follow the normal EVP questioning pattern. Be sure to compensate for extraneous sounds and normal location noise pollution. A genuine EVP of quality should provide for no question as to who said it. If it sounds like a fellow team member or a voice from outside, then it probably is. A good rule of thumb, if it's questionable, it's not evidence.

DVR Footage

DVR cameras should be placed in the optimum areas to capture activity. Trigger objects should be placed in view of these cameras. If an audio recorder or wireless microphone is to be left unattended, it is best to also place them in camera view as they can later be cross-referenced easily should any question arise to the validity of captured evidence.

All cameras, both still and video, should always be placed on tripods to decrease shakiness, blurriness, and many other types of non-paranormal abnormalities. If you are using a standard IR camera you should be able to capture any object movement or manipulation quite easily. Shadows and apparitions that lurk on the fringes of the IR beams may also be noted but are a very rare find indeed. If your team is equipped with a full spectrum camera you may capture balls of lights that are theorized to be collapsing energy fields. You may also capture faces and apparitions that have been seen appearing within the UV fields. Be sure to note the correct time code while reviewing the DVR system so that it will be easy to find and to present to your team and, if deemed as evidence, to your client.

Mini DV

The handheld video camera gives the person reviewing it the benefit of looking for visual evidence while also listening for EVPs. This can be very useful as it may sometimes back up an EVP that was captured on an audio recorder or give an alternative angle to something captured in a still or DVR camera. This angle may help to back up a piece of evidence or disprove it, depending on the situation.

They are also used visually to document changes on handheld thermometers and EMF type field meters alike.

Data Loggers

Having the ability to look back and see what the readings were throughout the case can be beneficial to backing up claims of paranormal activity. When used properly in combination with slated video and audio recorders, a data logger can go a long way to beef up the case for a haunting.

Still Photographs

It takes a very keen eye to filter through the numerous photographs that are taken during an investigation. Methodically search each one for the slightest abnormality, the faintest of shadow, or fluctuation of light. Comparing and contrasting photographs can be very time consuming, but the rewards are also very rich.

Common pitfalls that have swamped amateur investigators and professionals alike are:

- IR reflections
- Lanyards or camera straps in front of the lens
- Bugs in the field of the camera's vision
- Mists due to humidity, steam or hot water
- Cigarette smoke
- Hot breathe in cold air
- Condensation
- Simple glass reflection and refraction

Many of these pitfalls can be avoided by simply using the right equipment, using tripods, not using flash photography, and by being aware of and understanding your environment.

If you do believe you have captured an image of an apparition – a face or a ball of light – it is very important to study the image again carefully, looking for changes in light sources from previous photographs that could have caused a reflection or shift in shadows. The slightest movement by another investigator in the room or in the doorway is enough to alter the outcome of a single photograph, so be sure you know where everyone was at the time and where the IR lights, flashlights, and cameras were pointing at the time.

Can it be recreated? Take the camera back to the location if possible and recreate the same circumstances that were present at the time to the best of your knowledge and then take some shots. Vary the intensity of light, move the light, move the other cameras that were present, and take more shots. Compare these shots with the photo in question to see if you can come up with a logical explanation for what you have captured or if it is truly something from beyond.

Gathering up your evidence, reviewing it with your team, and coming to a shared opinion of the facts and your findings is your next task. Always be respectful of your fellow teammates, their ideas, and their opinions. You are not always going to see eye-to-eye with everyone, nor will you share the same feelings upon what is evidence and what is not. How you best handle those situations is up to you and the people in your group. Being willing to listen to one another and to look at things through alternative viewpoints can go a long way in easing team relations.

Once all is said and done, call upon your client to discuss the results of your investigation (see more in the Understanding Your Clients Chapter).

Don't be discouraged if your results come up short of your expectations. Honing your skills, finding alternative explanations, and putting peoples' minds at ease can often be just as rewarding as capturing evidence of the paranormal. Furthermore, it is important to be able to see every outcome as a positive one that will further fuel your desire to keep in the hunt, to further the science, and to bring humanity one step closer to finding the answer to that elusive question, "What happens after we die?"

Chapter 11

Comfort and Clarity

Talking with Your Client

*"Maturity is the ability to express one's own feelings
and convictions balanced with consideration for
the thoughts and feelings of others."*

HRAND SAXENAN

When all is said and done with the investigation and you and your team have reviewed and discussed the evidence, only then do you approach your client with your findings and your understanding of the reported occurrences.

We cannot stress enough how important it is to be clear in your descriptions and the relaying of your evidence to the client.

It is sometimes useful to also bring some pieces of equipment with you if they gathered some sort of evidence during the case. As an example, showing the client what a TriField meter is, how it works and how it was used in your case, can give them something tangible to help them better understand what it is you are talking about.

Be sure to be precise in reporting any activity as it pertains to what happened, where it happened and what your theory on it is.

Give them time to respond and share their thoughts and feelings on your findings.

If you were able to offer alternative explanations to some of the claims, it is important to demonstrate those alternatives and discuss them.

Remember that some clients are very attached to their beliefs of what is going on, so do not always expect them to be happy with you giving them a logical explanation. Do not get angry if they confront you, simply explain your points and your theories; do not criticize their theories or beliefs. A person that committed to something being paranormal will be hard pressed to admit it is anything else.

Alternatively, telling someone that they do have spirit activity or evidence of the paranormal in their home or workspace can also be very difficult for them to accept and understand.

Being caring, patient and informative is very important when dealing with an emotional client. Especially if you have found evidence of a close personal friend, family member or loved one, as you can imagine the impact that would have on someone whom is bereaved.

Do your best to answer every question that your client has and be sure to be truthful above all else. If you do not know the answer simply say that you do not know.

It can be very dangerous to go out on a limb with a theory and have other people hanging on it.

Once you have outlined for your client your investigation results and discussed thoroughly the intricacies of your findings see if there is anything you can do to help them. Discuss if a further investigation or follow up visit is warranted.

If you have identified Poltergeist activity, discuss with them the possible causes of such. Help them to understand the nature of a Residual if they have that type of activity.

Explain to them what to do with an Intelligent Spirit and discuss the intentions of the spirit if you have garnered any evidence to support it being peaceful or malevolent.

In the unfortunate case of an ill-willed Inhuman, speak with them about the various banishment techniques that they can try and offer to put them in contact with professionals whom offer these services if you know of any.

(For more information on dealing with all matters of spirit activity as have been outlined in this book please refer back to Chapter One)

When all is said and done, and your client has no more questions to ask or topics to discuss, thank them for trusting you to investigate their location, extend your services to them in the future and ask them to please refer you to anyone they know who may be experiencing paranormal activity.

Building a solid reputation in the community and the paranormal field is paramount if you wish to establish yourself as a seasoned, credible and trusted investigator.

In Closing Thoughts

"Begin doing what you want to do now.
We have only this moment, sparkling like a star in
our hand -- and melting like a snowflake."

MARIE BEYON RAY

Looking back through the pages of what we have written, reminiscing on that cold day in France when we first spoke of putting together a field guide combining the metaphysical understanding of the paranormal field and the scientific approach to it, there is an incredible feeling of accomplishment.

It is still important to understand the importance of being strong spiritually, regardless of what god or goddess to which you may or may not subscribe. Being of the right mindset and remaining in a positive place full of light, love, and peace are imperative to your success, not only in this field, but also in all walks of life.

The human body is a remarkable piece of equipment and, if looked after, like any piece of equipment, will last and perform for years. The clues to environmental patterns that are picked up by the body are huge. Life on this planet is far from separate. We are all connected on some level and the human body is a remarkable antenna for such amazing and subtle changes.

J.B. Rhine of Duke University began tests on Extra Sensory Perception (ESP) in the 1930s, which reflect the biofeedback experiments of modern day, and many of his experiments continue today with some very interesting results. The human mind is an unfathomed tool, which is still very much unexplored; its mysteries are still very much behind the veil as the spirits we seek to meet.

Nelya Mikhailova a, Russian-born woman, was quiet capable of moving objects on command using only the power of her mind. Edward Naumov, a biologist from Moscow State University, was one of the first to observe this inside a lab environment and it is reported that she displayed some enthralling results.

Pavel Stepanek was a Czech student that showed amazing results when tested inside a lab displaying wonderful scores when using the classic ESP card pack, designed with a mixed set of simple images that the subject must predict before each one is turned over -- a process known as the focusing effect.

Peter Hurkos was a Dutch man who was approached by police stationed at The Hague. He only had to hold the coat of the dead man before continuing to describe the murderer in detail, including glasses, moustache, and a wooden leg. Police confirmed they had arrested a man fitting the description and Hurkos went on to tell the police where they could find the murder weapon.

Stories such as these circulate the world on a daily basis and show us there are a class of people who are able to sense the Earth's pulse, otherwise known as ley lines, a series of natural energy grids that circumvent the Earth's surface. An article in New Scientist magazine, published in 1987, suggested that species as diverse as pigeons, whales, bees, and even bacteria can navigate using the Earth's magnetic field. We have GPS systems to guide us from A to point B, but the obvious question is, "What have we lost in our drive to break nature's back?"

Be aware of your thoughts, of your mental state, and of your true intentions. Be guarded, but do not lock away your emotions and you heart. Only in the true alignment of a healthy mind, body and soul, can we hope to live a full and successful life.

Personal Remarks

In finishing I must acknowledge I have never been that metaphorical sheep -- I will not follow the flock. I'm too much of a free thinker and will continue to be so. Trying to understanding both sides of this intricate topic of the paranormal can make life much more interesting as nothing is ever black and white.

This book was not designed to be artistic with picture fillers; it was designed as a guide to those in the paranormal field who wanted information to help their investigations. Don't be a member of the flock, use this book as a guide and venture, live and experience. Readers will no doubt experience slight changes in what we have written but the core I hope will stay the same.

Barry FitzGerald

Personal Remarks

I would just once again like to stress my main reason for being involved in this field, which is to shed some light on the existence of the afterlife. Not to prove or disprove any specific religion, but solely to bring forth a greater understanding of how we are all connected in this world and how each of our actions, no matter how mundane, affects the lives of others, generations to come, and the very fabric of the Universe.

It is my hope that by making people aware of an existence beyond this one, we will as a society become less self-centered and self focused; that we will learn to live for the greater good, to take care of one other, and treat everyone with the kindness, compassion, and respect that we all deserve.

In the end, I am just trying to do my part to fix the world, one act of kindness at a time.

Thanks for reading -- Tikkun Olam for life.

Dustin J. Pari

LaVergne, TN USA
29 September 2009
159292LV00003B/160/P